W9-AEX-649

Daughters of Time

Daughters of Time

Creating Woman's Voice in Southern Story

❧❦❧

Lucinda H. MacKethan

Mercer University Lamar Memorial Lectures No. 32

The University of Georgia Press   Athens and London

© 1990 by the University of Georgia Press
Athens, Georgia 30602
All rights reserved

Designed by Erin Kirk
Set in Linotron Berkeley Old Style Medium
The paper in this book meets the guidelines
for permanence and durability of the Committee on
Production Guidelines for Book Longevity of the
Council on Library Resources.

Printed in the United States of America

94 93 92 91 90   5 4 3 2 1

Library of Congress Cataloging in Publication Data

MacKethan, Lucinda Hardwick.
Daughters of time: creating woman's voice in southern
story / Lucinda H. MacKethan.
p.   cm.—(Mercer University Lamar memorial lectures;
no. 32)
Bibliography: p.
Includes index.
ISBN 0-8203-1169-3 (alk. paper)
1. American fiction—Southern States—History and
criticism.   2. American fiction—Women authors—
History and criticism.   3. Women and literature—
Southern States.   4. Southern States in literature.
5. Women in literature.   I. Title.   II. Series: Lamar
memorial lectures; no. 32.
PS261.M24   1990
813'.0099287—dc20   89-4824
                                                     CIP

British Library Cataloging in Publication Data available

This book is dedicated to my mother

EMILY DOWNTON HARDWICK

"The quality of the mother's life—

however embattled and unprotected—

is her primary bequest to her daughter."

CONTENTS

Foreword

ix

Preface

xi

Introduction: Southern Daughters of Time

1

ONE ⌣

Naming the Father: The Stories of Catherine Hammond
and Harriet Jacobs

15

TWO

Prodigal Daughters: The Journeys of Ellen Glasgow,
Zora Neale Hurston, and Eudora Welty

37

THREE

The Voice in the Garden: Creating Women
in the Modern Southern Novel

64

Postscript: Writing Letters Home

98

Notes

113

Works Cited

121

Index

125

FOREWORD

Lucinda Hardwick MacKethan's visit to Mercer University in October 1988 to deliver the annual Lamar Memorial Lectures was awaited with much anticipation on the part of students, faculty, and townspeople interested in the culture of the American South. A number of previous lecturers had incorporated the study of women into their examinations of southern culture, and one had gone a step further to make women the focus of his analysis of a fascinating aspect of southern history, the single-tax colony at Fairhope, Alabama. Never before, however, had a Lamar lecturer dealt with southern women's literature as a discrete subject. What's more, for the first time, the Lamar lecturer was a woman.

Anticipation resulted in a packed lecture hall. (Whoever invented folding chairs is greatly to be praised.) The audience at each of the three lectures was eager to hear the voice of a southern woman scholar describe the "voice" of southern women writers. No one left disappointed. Examining the quest for autonomous selfhood in the fiction and nonfiction of southern women writers, black and white, Professor MacKethan stressed the interplay of region, race, and gender as springs of identity from antebellum days to our own time. Because of the format of the lectures, the audiences did not have the pleasure of listening to Professor MacKethan's postscript, a poignant essay in its own right, which she describes herein as "a way of ending what one hates to end." We at Mercer share that sentiment. We hated to see her lectures end, but we rejoice that they are now available in book form. We believe that *Daughters of Time* is a major contribution to the growing field of southern women's studies.

For more than thirty years, the benevolence of the late Eugenia Dorothy Blount Lamar has made possible this lecture series. Professor MacKethan has served well Mrs. Lamar's goal to encourage in the study of southern culture "the very highest type of scholarship." Mercer University is exceedingly fortunate to have had Lucinda Hardwick Mac-Kethan, a scholar and speaker of the first order, as the Lamar lecturer for 1988.

Wayne Mixon
for the
Lamar Memorial Lectures Committee

PREFACE

In the course of putting together a series of lectures on "Woman's Voice in Southern Story," I could not help but be conscious of and deeply grateful for the voice and the vision of one particular southern woman, Eugenia Dorothy Blount Lamar, whose dedication to southern life and culture led her to establish the Lamar Memorial Lecture Series at Mercer University. The series, through the diligence of the men and women of the Lamar Memorial Lectures Committee, has honored her ideal while providing all of us who study and love the South with a cavalcade of valuable resources in the books that grow from the lectures. To be included among the company of scholars who have given these lectures has provided me with the one experience that truly deserves my children's favorite adjective—*awesome* is the word. I thank the members of the committee for this challenging opportunity to explore new territory, to share ideas with wonderfully receptive audiences, and to try out my own voice in an ideal setting.

This book represents, in slightly expanded form and with the addition of a postscript, the lectures as I presented them during the three beautiful October days that I was a guest of Mercer University. As essays they reflect the nature of the original occasion. Catherine Hammond, Harriet Jacobs, Ellen Glasgow, Zora Neale Hurston, Eudora Welty, Alice Walker, and Lee Smith are women whom I have studied, taught to my students, and written about separately over the last several years. The lectures, and this book, gave me the opportunity to bring these writers together in order to make discoveries, to fashion connections, and to listen throughout as closely as I could to what they have to say. From different racial, class, and historical perspectives, they have stories in common to tell —about themselves, about their achievement of voice, and about their visions of the South. The time constraints of the lecture format and my desire to appeal to many different angles of interest made it impossible for me to review extensively or to synthesize the ever-enlarging body of scholarship in the area of southern women's studies. Since the publication of Ann Firor Scott's groundbreaking work, *Southern Lady: From Pedestal to Politics, 1830–1930* (1970), many valuable books and articles have appeared. I hope that the assumptions that underlie my readings of southern women's letters, autobiographies, and novels accurately reflect pertinent evidence that literary scholars and historians have brought forward, especially in the last decade, on this subject. I have tried to fit many different kinds of sources into my study, which attempts, first and foremost, to trace the process of self-creation that southern women embarked upon when they began to speak, through a variety of written forms of expression, about their experiences, their hopes, and their memories.

To the Lamar Memorial Lectures Committee, who invited me to appear as the thirty-second speaker in this series, I again express my gratitude. To Henry Warnock, professor emeritus of history at Mercer, and to his wife Patricia, I add my thanks for sharing their time and their beautiful city with me. And I wish I could think of some especially grand way to show my appreciation to Wayne Mixon, who makes the difficult job of chairing the Lectures Committee look easy, and to Fran Mixon, who knows exactly how to make a nervous visitor feel not only welcome but at home. Sammye C. Greer, dean of the College of Liberal Arts, as well as many faculty, students, and friends of Mercer University, offered insights and suggestions that have found their way into these essays and demonstrated what a lively spirit of inquiry thrives on their campus. In particular, Sharon D. Lee, a teacher at Perry (Georgia) High School, helped by sharing an illuminating paper she has written on *One Writer's Beginnings*.

There are others to thank as well. The English department at North Carolina State University granted a semester's released time from teaching so that I could work on the lectures. I began my study of Harriet Jacobs during my year at the National Humanities Center, where an exceptionally fine library staff provided able and cheerful assistance. An NEH Summer Seminar on autobiography, conducted by James Olney, marked the beginning of an interest in autobiographies that is still absorbing. Louis D. Rubin, Jr., who at Hollins College was the first person to encourage me to find my own voice, has continued to offer that encouragement for, heaven forbid, a quarter of a century. Students in my Southern Writers classes at N.C. State have always been some of my best teachers. And Robbie Knott, once a student, now a colleague, friend, and critic, read draft after draft and always found the right way to tell me what was working and what wasn't. At home, daughter Karen, son Alex, and husband John cheered me on and helped me to keep things in perspective. At the University of Georgia Press, Karen Orchard, executive editor, and Angela G. Ray, editor, were generous with their encouragement, and Mary Drake McFeely provided invaluable assistance in copyediting.

In reading stories of daughters' places within their families, I have been remembering my own. I am lucky to have a brother, Pearce, and a sister, Dana, who like to remember along with me. I was lucky, too, to have a father, Lewis Eugene Hardwick, who passed along his love of books and the South. I am luckiest of all to have a mother to whom I here offer my deepest thanks, for giving me a model of courage, for making me laugh, and for listening.

Southern Daughters of Time

Daughters of Time, the hypocritic Days,
Muffled and dumb like barefoot dervishes,
And marching single in an endless file,
Bring diadems and fagots in their hands.
To each they offer gifts after his will,
Bread, kingdoms, stars, and sky that holds them all.
I, in my pleached garden, watched the pomp,
Forgot my morning wishes, hastily
Took a few herbs and apples, and the Day
Turned and departed silent. I, too late,
Under her solemn fillet saw the scorn.

My idea for this book came about through voices, the voices of southern women storytellers who, in my personal experience as well as in many of my favorite books, have helped me to discover who I am. I still hear my grandmother's Kentucky voice; as we sat on her front porch in the summer, glasses of iced lemonade in hand, she would explain to her exiled granddaughter who belonged to what family, who had married which cousin, and how I fit into the family tree—everyone was a cousin, as it turned out, everyone who mattered. I have tried to keep my mother's voice; her letters to me, beginning the year that I left home to go eight hundred miles away to college, now fill three boxes that hold twenty-five years of our long-distance sharing. And now, teaching a course called

"Southern Writers," I sometimes ask my students if they can hear their own lives, as I hear mine, echoing in the stories of women who wrote themselves into being. One of the voices that makes us listen belongs to Eudora Welty's Edna Earle Ponder. In *The Ponder Heart,* Edna Earle tells stories, nonstop, about her Uncle Daniel, the heir to her family's fortune and the sadly inadequate standardbearer of the family name and reputation. The stories wind on and on as Edna Earle sits with an un-named, and we suspect uncomfortable, stranger who has wandered into the lobby of her deserted boarding house, the Beulah Hotel, in the small town of Clay, Mississippi. At one point in her narrative Edna Earle de-scribes Uncle Daniel as a prodigious storyteller: "He took every soul I let in at the Beulah straight to his heart. 'Hello, son—what's news?'—then he'd start in. Oh, the stories! He made free with everybody's—he'd tell yours and his and the Man in the Moon's. Not mine: he wouldn't dream I had one, he loves me so—but everybody else's" (70).

In this one statement, Edna Earle seems to relegate herself to the fate common to so many southern women—the position of silent servant. This spinster narrator lived all her life in the reflected glory of her eccen-tric Uncle Daniel, whose freedom to roam, to enjoy exciting escapades, including two marriages, left her storyless in his shadow. Charged by her grandfather with the task of keeping Uncle Daniel out of trouble, Edna Earle presents herself as the dutiful daughter whose sole function is the protection of the wayward male heir. At the Beulah Hotel, she became a kind of procurer of victims for Uncle Daniel's obsessive storytelling assaults. And yet never was she included in the plots that his stories unfolded. As woman kin, and in the name of "love," she existed for both Uncle Daniel and Grandfather only as caretaker, never as creator of her own stories or even as a character in the stories of others.

The Ponder Heart looks like a traditional tall tale of a propertied south-ern male who romps through life with a worshipful woman behind him to set everything right in the end. But looks are deceiving, as is usually the case with Welty's comic works. What we are asked to do is to listen, for the sound of the voice telling the story becomes the primary story. Edna Earle Ponder ends up taking Uncle Daniel's voice, and his story, away from him. While she portrays herself within the narrative as the womanly, sacrificing giver—"I don't try, myself, to make people happy," she says, "I just try to give them what they think they want"—she owns, after all, the only voice we hear in this book. At the story's end, Uncle Daniel is curiously, deadly silent in his upstairs room, while Edna Earle takes over his pastime and his identity. When she says, "The sight of a stranger was always meat and drink to him. The stranger don't have to open his mouth. Uncle Daniel is ready to do all the talking," we are aware that we are the trapped stranger listening to Edna Earle doing all the talking. As Edna Earle launches into her narrative, she warns her captive audience that "if you read, you'll put your eyes out. Let's just talk" (11). The message is to those reading as well—this narrator wants no other stories but her own, and when she says talk, what she means is listen. The transformation of Edna Earle the niece and granddaughter, who exists to give and protect, into Edna Earle the storyteller, completely in control of both her male "subject" and her listener, provides the ironic underpinning of this tall tale. Her narrative is in a way a wonderfully vengeful tour de force: Uncle Daniel never dreamed she had a story, yet in the end, hers is the only one we hear.

The Ponder Heart is, finally, a story about woman kin as storyteller and about the creative function of authorship for woman in a society that traditionally denied her a story of her own. Edna Earle steals the storyteller's craft from the male practitioner, which is why her name is part of Welty's strategy. As Welty pointed out in *One Writer's Beginnings*, the name Edna Earle was often given to southern girls as a testament to the heroine of one of the South's most "wildly popular" novels, Augusta Jane Evans's *St. Elmo*. Published in 1866, *St. Elmo* was the story of an Edna Earl (even though the title refers to the male lead character) who, Welty tells us, "succeeded in bringing a dissolute, sinning roué and atheist of a lover (St. Elmo) to his knees" (*OWB* 7). Evans's Edna Earl was also a successful writer of highly moral stories who denounced woman's suffrage and in the end, accepted the reformed St. Elmo as her husband. The novel ends with this poem that he addresses to his noble Edna: "Accomplish thou my manhood, and thyself / Lay thy sweet hands in mine and trust to me." Anne Goodwyn Jones, commenting on these lines, points out that "By trusting her husband to navigate the 'wild,' Edna will survive; by 'accomplish[ing his] manhood,' she will give him an identity" (91). The woman author takes on what Evans herself undoubtedly saw as a more womanly role, that of making her man's life complete by giving him total power over her own destiny. Welty tells us that her mother was "able to forgo" this book that seemed a staple in other southern home libraries, but that Mrs. Welty "remembered the classic advice given to rose growers on how to water their bushes long enough: 'Take a chair and *St. Elmo*'" (*OWB* 7). The image of sturdy southern ladies of the turn of the century watering their flowers, tending to their gardens, with part of their energies while also absorbing the story of the strong-minded but self-sacrificial model, Edna Earle, is one that tells its own story of women's sense of their place in Welty's world.

Welty's Edna Earle is conscious of "woman's place," so part of her story is her silence concerning her lack of status in that place. Yes, she steals Uncle Daniel's show, but the costs are the dark side of this comedy. What Edna Earle wants, she cannot say: a home of her own, a story that does not have to be stolen, a creative life that does not depend on menfolk for its validity. Edna Earle gave me rich tones of talking and also dark spaces of silence to use as I began to define for myself the southern woman's storytelling voice. In large part through my reading of southern women writers, the word "voice" has come to have for me, as it has for many women, a metaphorical dimension, encompassing all that goes into the expression of unique selfhood. As the authors of *Women's Ways of Knowing* learned when they interviewed women for their study, "women repeatedly used the metaphor of voice to depict their intellectual and ethical development; . . . voice, mind, and self were intricately intertwined."[1] When the messages of my "voices" began to combine into similar refrains and patterns, I found a name for them in a familiar Emerson poem: these women, inheriting a cultural ideal of feminine identity that sentenced them to silence, became "Daughters of Time."

Emerson's poem "Days," which personifies the days of the week as "Daughters of Time," evokes the exacting pain connected to the artist's choice of his calling. In the past, when we read the poem in my classes, I hoped that students would wonder whether the "morning wishes" that the poet forgot were really the important ones—did he deserve the Day's scorn for taking merely "herbs and apples"? Only recently have I come to look upon Emerson's quiet and uncharacteristic expression of self-doubt with eyes for the irony of his image of the "Days" that brought him opportunities and options as a man and a poet. He quite naturally, I now suppose, pictured the Days as feminine daughters of Father Time, quite naturally saw his choices as being offered by serving girls who made no sound, quite naturally used only the masculine pronoun as he noted who was to be offered their gifts. In other words, he quite naturally limited the choice of the artist's calling to men. Muffled, dumb, barefoot, bearing gifts, departing silently, Emerson's serving maids typify his ideal of woman and the ideal of his culture as well.[2] How aware, I wonder, was he of the implications of his poem's last line? There the Day who takes the poet's "order" makes no sound, having neither power nor will to tell him what to choose, yet her scorn is unveiled nonetheless.

In this study we will listen to women telling stories of their lives in the South. The stories concern a culture that remained patriarchal even longer than other regions of America; thus, the women who tell them begin with the voices, the identities, the constraints of daughterhood.[3] Southern daughters were the creations and inheritors of a culture which in part defined and perpetuated itself by their silence. The question for a would-be woman storyteller schooled in this ideal of feminine identity was, as Louise Westling phrases it, "How could a person brought up to be soft and yielding, warm and self-sacrificing, dare to intrude herself upon the public mind? How could she presume?" (54). Yet strategies of "presumption" could be, had to be, found. Emerson's servant daughters did find a way to communicate the scorn hidden under their solemn veils. Edna Earle did appropriate a story that Uncle Daniel never dreamed she had. My study concerns the possibilities for reversal, for empowerment, that southern women seized upon when they moved beyond the role of daughter and into the role of storyteller. Central to my exploration of this direction are certain questions: what does the entity of Daughter entail? what "veiled" strategies does a woman bring to the mission of voicing herself in male gardens? can she take possession of her own garden, a place where she is free to imagine, to design, to produce creations that bear her distinctive personality and purpose? how, ultimately, does she speak a story out of the condition of voicelessness? In the face of conclusive evidence that women's right to growth into autonomous selfhood was delayed even more strenuously in the South than in other regions, the surprising news is that the South's daughters of time did make just such stories, prolifically. I begin with the certainty that southern literature is graced by the remarkably strong presence of women storytellers, black and white, who in autobiographies and in fictional narratives address specifically their determination to become, freely, themselves through creative acts of voicing.

My design for presenting the women writers whom I identify as "Daughters of Time" involves a three-part examination that is divided both chronologically and by genre. First, I will look at the letters of a plantation wife and the autobiography of a female slave in order to analyze their revisions of the standard portrait of the white patriarch. In hearing their voices, we meet the women who were in all respects the "housekeepers" for the antebellum South's exclusive exponent of power. The plantation wife is Catherine Hammond, married to South Carolina politician and intellectual James Henry Hammond; Catherine wrote her story in letters so self-effacing that they come close to eradicating the voice that makes its plea within them. The slave is Harriet Jacobs, who grew up as a slave of Dr. James Norcom in Edenton, North Carolina, and finally escaped to New York when she was twenty-nine. Her autobiography, *Incidents in the Life of a Slave Girl* (1861), is a remarkable testament to woman's will to break the silence that the patriarchal institution of slavery imposed through both racial and sexual dominance.

In part 2, I will trace the process through which three twentieth-century southern daughters, living in a South that still enshrined a system of patriarchal dominance, became writers. The voices that we hear in this section project the autobiographical personas of Ellen Glasgow, Zora Neale Hurston, and Eudora Welty. The journey to self-definition, centered in struggles to find and master a new language, comprises both the direction and the parameters of Glasgow's *The Woman Within* (1954), Hurston's *Dust Tracks on a Road* (1942), and Welty's *One Writer's Beginnings* (1984). In their autobiographies, all three writers operated from a consciousness of an inward self that directed them to words and stories as a means of knowing and living in the world. They began their quests clearly defined as daughters, yet in their journeys from and returns to southern homeplaces, they became creators, developing a tradition of strong woman's voice in southern writing. Although they represent differing racial, geographic, educational, and class perspectives, their similar experiences as daughters in southern communities set against their similar visions of themselves as storytellers demonstrate how gender and culture can affect woman's creating a sense of herself as writer.

In part 3, I will relate some of the strategies of self-definition and self-completion that Glasgow, Hurston, and Welty named in their auto-biographies to the essential search that informs one key novel by each woman: Glasgow's *Barren Ground* (1925), Hurston's *Their Eyes Were Watching God* (1937), and Welty's *The Optimist's Daughter* (1972). In my readings of these novels I will emphasize the concept of character as agent for change and the value of storymaking in the creation of self. Laurel McKelva of *The Optimist's Daughter,* like Glasgow's Dorinda Oakley and Hurston's Janie Crawford, starts out with a sense of family identity that holds her within the contours of patriarchal, parental expectations. Yet all three of these characters are forced to challenge and to change their roles as the preservers and products of tradition; in acts of creative self-expression, they change themselves, their communities, and those who listen to their stories. A brief postscript looks at women characters, Alice Walker's Celie, from *The Color Purple* (1982), and Lee Smith's Ivy Rowe, from *Fair and Tender Ladies* (1988), whose stories reflect not only the quests patterned in earlier southern novels but also the changing circumstances affecting women's writing in our own era. In these two contemporary novels the characters quite literally write themselves into being through letters that celebrate motherhood and daughterhood but, most importantly, sisterhood as the defining connection for women's experience within southern families.

Each of the three parts of my study is dominated by a figure that helped me to organize my perceptions of the writers I have selected: first the patriarch, then the daughter, and finally the novelist. As I look at the writing and the silences of Catherine Hammond and Harriet Jacobs, I will interpret the critical role that the concept of patriarchy has played historically in defining southern women's identity and destiny. Two interlocking assumptions direct my conceptualization of the way the patriarchal system in the slaveholding South circumscribed women's attempts at self-definition. First, the patriarchal structure of the antebel-lum plantation family insured that women in the South would wait much longer than their northern sisters for a time in which their society would look favorably upon their goal of autonomous selfhood. This assertion has been amply documented in several recent histories. Bertram Wyatt-Brown, who in *Southern Honor* (1982) extensively explored women's place in a culture shaped by a male code, concluded that while familial relations in the North and the South were "very similar" in the pre-Civil War period, "antebellum Yankee women, at least those in the upper and middle classes, had begun to question, with increasing insistence, their age-old subjection"; their southern sisters, on the other hand, were the wives and daughters and slaves of men who, as Wyatt-Brown puts it, expected to remain patriarchs "eternally" and who thus held tenaciously to ideals for women that kept them in their subservient place (226).

Two women historians have been much less tentative than Wyatt-Brown in their assessment of the effects of patriarchy on southern women's progress to freedom. Catherine Clinton, in *The Plantation Mistress* (1982), writes unequivocally that "feminist ideology, nascent in the post-Revolutionary North and destined to emerge vigorously at mid-century, lay dormant throughout most of the nineteenth century in the South" (205). More recently, Jean Friedman, in *The Enclosed Garden* (1985), asserts that "because the South continued what was essentially an older agrarian and family-oriented structural pattern," antebellum southern women "were deprived of a social basis for reform" that northern women found available in urban environments which modernized and broke down patriarchal boundaries much earlier (7). Her study of what she calls "the southern evangelical community" crosses racial lines to explore the effects of patriarchally defined family and church discipline upon both white and Afro-American women of the nineteenth-century South, for she finds many of the same limitations operating for women of both races.

The work of Clinton and Friedman has encouraged me in my resolve to bring white and Afro-American women together in my exploration of woman's voice in southern story. My second assumption concerning the effect of the South's patriarchal structure relates to the question of race in its explicit connection to gender in the South: although white and Afro-American women endured separate experiences of bondage and silence within the patriarchal South, gender identity provided many similar strategies for meeting the threat to selfhood. Minrose Gwin tells us in *Black and White Women of the Old South* (1985) that "within the patriarchal system," the slave woman and the plantation mistress "were thrust into diametrically opposed but mutually dependent roles" (48). Both served the ideological and sexual purposes of the master, who used the position of patriarch to exercise complete control over their bodies and their definitions of themselves. The "sexual dynamics of slavery," as Catherine Clinton calls it, shaped patriarchs who would "tolerate no interference in their reproductive domain" (205). Thus while the slave woman was classified as "whore" and the lady was "always chaste" in the patriarch's sexual lexicon, in fact both white and black women were means to the patriarchal end of producing either legitimate heirs or marketable chattel.

Hazel Carby, in *Reconstructing Womanhood: The Emergence of the Afro-American Woman Novelist* (1987), stresses the differences, rather than the similarities, inherent in the patriarch's relations to the black and white women whom he controlled. She makes the point that the ideology of true womanhood that governed patriarchal definitions "excluded black women from the category 'women'" (40). However, she too sees that ideologies of white southern womanhood and black womanhood were controlled by "different but interdependent codes of sexuality" in the antebellum South (20). My emphasis falls on the points where the gender interests of white and black women intersect to create similar expressions of growth into voice, that expression of unique mind and selfhood. Clinton tells us, for instance, of a plantation mistress who wrote to her husband, "You have it in your power to enjoy company where you please. . . . But here I am shut up like a canary bird" (179). The slave Harriet Jacobs wrote in her autobiography of the same period, "I was twenty-one years in that cage of obscene birds" (52). There can be no downplaying the difference in the experiences that led these women to the metaphor of the caged bird. They make different points in using it to strike out at the white patriarch. However, the fact that both women turned to this metaphoric means of expressing their situation makes comparisons valuable. Deborah White points out in *Ar'n't I A Woman? Female Slaves in the Plantation South* (1985) that "in the antebellum South, . . . ideas about women went hand in hand with ideas about race. Women and blacks were the foundation on which Southern white

males built their patriarchal regime" (58). As I explore the writings of a
slave and a plantation mistress, my position will be that both white and
Afro-American women served a master who, though he defined them dif-
ferently, sentenced them both to silence as he designed a domain which
would allow him absolute authority through his position as Father.

When I move, in the second section, to consider Ellen Glasgow, Zora
Neale Hurston, and Eudora Welty as three writers who successfully
wrote their way out of the cage of southern patriarchy, assumptions
concerning the figure of the daughter will be essential to my analysis.
My proposition here is that what we can call the "daughter's sensibility" could become an enabling perception for the southern woman
who sought to claim voice through writing within and about her father's
house.[4] She could use her position in ways that transformed southern
patriarchy from a stifling cage into an open window on the world. Certain traditionally southern ways of seeing when combined with woman's
ways of knowing could give the daughter-writer access to voice and
power within her culture. For our purposes I will outline only in very
general terms the qualities of a southern way of seeing that the women
writers in this study embody in their fiction: first, respect for family as
the heart of social order; next, the symbolization of the home as the
locus of all inheritable values; third, the tension between hate and love
for the father, who in the culture holds the power to define, to validate,
to circumscribe, and to disinherit; and finally, acceptance of memory as
the primary means of knowing and conscious selection of what Lewis
Simpson has called a "southern aesthetic of memory" as a means of
organizing perception.[5]

Glasgow, Hurston, and Welty draw upon these traditionally southern perceptual tendencies. They enlarge upon them, however, through
"women's ways of knowing," an expression that is the title of a book
which has helped me to shape my definition of woman's voice. In
Women's Ways of Knowing (1986), Mary Belenky, Blythe Clinchy, Nancy
Goldberger, and Jill Tarule examine "five different perspectives from
which women view reality and draw conclusions about truth, knowledge, and authority" (3). These perspectives range from silence, to listening to the voices of others, to relying on the inner voice and undertaking the quest for self, to attending to the voice of reason and connected

knowing, to integrating the voices. These different ways of knowing appear in many common areas—far too many for me to begin to address here—among the writers we are viewing. The key point for my treatment is that, in their autobiographies, Glasgow, Hurston, and Welty undertake quests for self that start at the position of "subjective knowledge" and move to the position of "constructed knowledge." This last position belongs to women who "want to embrace all the pieces of the self in some ultimate sense of the whole—daughter, friend, mother, lover, nurturer, thinker, artist, advocate. They want to avoid what they perceive to be a shortcoming in many men—the tendency to compartmentalize thought and feeling, home and work, self and other. In women, there is an impetus to try to deal with life, internal and external, in all its complexity. And they want to develop a voice of their own to communicate to others their understanding of life's complexity" (137). To a great extent, this concept of "constructed knowledge" constitutes the dream of knowing that haunts, goads, tortures, inspires, and completes the writer's vision of Glasgow, Hurston, and Welty. Within rural southern settings, from the vantage point of daughters, these writers and the women characters through whom they voice the tension of their positions seek an integration of mind and place that both celebrates and transcends gender.

The cost to the writer who uses her daughterhood in the ways I have described is the threat of losing her secure position within the family that has identified and sustained her primary sense of who she is; the reward is artistic freedom and selfhood. Essential to each of the writers I consider in sections two and three is her determination to balance risk and reward, to effect separation and autonomy without sacrificing the vital sense of connectedness that roots her gender-identified roles of creator and nurturer. Carol Gilligan's *In a Different Voice* (1982) explains why the tension between what Welty has called "love and separateness" is so vital: "We know ourselves as separate only insofar as we live in connection with others, and . . . we experience relationship only insofar as we differentiate other from self" (63). It is true, as Joanne Frye says in *Living Stories, Telling Lives: Women and the Novel in Contemporary Experience* (1986), that "if she is to learn to say 'I' as a woman, [woman] must depart from her place as favored daughter in the patriarchal family" (49). Yet it is also true that her knowledge of that place, and her narrative reconstructions of it in story, provide the southern woman with a pathway to freedom that also allows a return to, or at least an accommodation of, the familial role. As I move in part 3 to consider the autobiographically based fiction of Glasgow, Hurston, and Welty, I will follow the stories of characters who, like their authors, travelled both away from and back to the father's house. When Dorinda Oakley, Janie Crawford, and Laurel McKelva return home, they confront and change their own and others' perceptions of traditional life patterns within their communities. Through the creation of these characters in stories set squarely within southern culture, Glasgow, Hurston, and Welty have been able to revolutionize our perceptions of women's possibilities in a patriarchally organized world.

In *Living Stories: Telling Lives,* Joanne Frye gives one explanation of why the novel form is important to the design of a "feminist poetics": the novel potentially sustains a significant "enabling power in yielding new understandings of women's lives" (47). In the third section of my study, I concentrate on some of the qualities of the novel form that Frye identifies in order to celebrate southern women's stories as a force for change. Frye theorizes that the novel form is not only "an agent of interpretation" but additionally "a possible agent of *re*interpretation, not only giving form but also altering accepted forms" (21). The accepted formulas for charting women's experience—romance, love, marriage—prescribed by patriarchal history are thus transformed and vitalized in what Alice Walker calls "mystor[ies]," stories of the way women know themselves.[6] Glasgow's *Barren Ground,* Hurston's *Their Eyes Were Watching God,* and Welty's *The Optimist's Daughter* qualify as this kind of story. Their characters Dorinda Oakley, Janie Crawford, and Laurel McKelva seek explicitly to revise the accepted forms by which they are known and thus to make knowing themselves their priority.

One of the chief values of Frye's work for my purposes is her discussion of character. As she says, the convention of character in the novel has been "particularly destructive for women" because it has traditionally tended toward "an enactment of the dominant culture's values" (41). Frye notes, however, that what she calls "the modernist reassessment of character" brings to the concept "the recognition that identity is a construct," so that the idea of character "becomes most prominently the expression of agency, the capacity to act toward change—an empirical being with experiential continuity over time, a proper name, a distinctive set of remembered experiences, and a group of attributes assigned to her or him by other characters or people and by the perceiving self, but above all one who acts, even beyond the limits of roles and labels" (42). Glasgow, Hurston, and Welty are women novelists who have participated fully in the "modernist reassessment of character," creating stories of women who learn to act on their perceptions and change their roles and labels. For these character-agents, different forms of storytelling become a primary agency of action: through dream, through active memory, or through conscious narrative shaping, Dorinda, Janie, and Laurel find their best means of conforming outward circumstance to inner definition of self. In selecting black and white southern women novelists who both exhibit their power of voicing in their vocation and take the attainment of it as their characters' central quest, I am focusing on daughters of time who have turned the father's house of fiction into mothers' gardens of lifegiving, freedom-singing story.

All of the women in my study went against cultural and familial expectations in risking the changes that their roles as storytellers demanded. In *Diving Deep and Surfacing: Women Writers on Spiritual Quest* (1986), Carol P. Christ mourns that "women live in a world where women's stories rarely have been told from their own perspectives. The stories celebrated in culture are told by men. Thus men have actively shaped their experiences of self and world, and their most profound stories orient them to what they perceive as the great powers of the universe. But since women have not told their own stories, they have not actively shaped their experiences of self and world nor named the great powers from their own perspectives" (4). This assessment, which hears women's silences more than their voices, takes us back to the image in Emerson's "Days" of daughters who bear and serve yet never assimilate or take for their own the father's creative gifts. Yet my own journey through the writing of southern women, from the real letters of Catherine Hammond to the fictional letters of Alice Walker's Celie and Lee Smith's Ivy Rowe, has shown me women who *have* told their own stories, often at great risk but always with fulfilling results. The daughters whose voices we will now hear found ways to name themselves and their experiences in a South that promoted men's versions of culture more radically and for a longer time than other regions. These writers, within the context of southern literary tradition, offer richly varied answers and dramatic possibilities to the question, "How does your garden grow?" They have defined themselves as southerners and as daughters, not without ambivalence but without scorn; they have dealt with Time—with both human change and patriarchally controlled history—as a worthy challenger; and they have lived and made their living through self-expression. In their extended stories, both autobiographical and fictional, the writers whose voices we hear have successfully brought themselves and a woman's world into creative presence.

CHAPTER ONE

Naming the Father

The Stories of Catherine Hammond
and Harriet Jacobs

In the slaveholding South, Bertram Wyatt-Brown tells us, "the mystique of names carried considerable meaning in the family and the community," more so than in the free states.[1] Like Adam in the Garden of Eden, the southern patriarch defined his world through his power to name: wife, children, slaves, animals, and homesites testified to their owner's pride in possession. William Byrd of Westover, one of the South's earliest and most successful patriarchs, explained the basis for the slaveholder's power to name in a letter to the Earl of Orrery written in 1726: "I have a large Family of my own," he boasted. "Like one of the Patriarchs, I have my Flocks and my Herds, my Bondsmen and Bondswomen."[2] Calling up the biblical model, Byrd shows that his sense of family is embedded in a sense of ownership; naming cemented this relationship. The gap between the slaveowner's vision and the vision that his wife or his slaves might hold is clearly expressed in the diary of Mary Boykin Chesnut, wife of James Chesnut, Jr., whose father was one of South Carolina's wealthiest owners of land and slaves. In her diary entry for March 18, 1861, she writes: "Like the patriarchs of old our men live all in one house with their wives & their concubines & the Mulattoes one sees in every family exactly resemble the white children. . . . Mr. Harris said it was so patriarchal. So it is—flocks & herds & slaves—& wife Leah does not

suffice. Rachel must be *added,* if not *married.* & all the time they seem
to think themselves patterns—models of husbands and fathers" (Woodward and Muhlenfeld, 42–43). Chesnut, from the same biblical source
as Byrd, turns the tables on patriarchy, renaming the institution and its
practitioners from a decidedly different perspective.

In this chapter, following Mary Boykin Chesnut's lead, we will bear
witness to how other antebellum women undermined the patriarch's
power to name his Rachels, his Leahs, and their children, black and
white. By *naming,* I mean defining; naming, by extension, assumes this
kind of significance—the right to name proffers the right to determine
identity and fate. The southern patriarch exclusively held this right. In
his official histories, plantation ledgers, and framed genealogies, he announced his mastery as he marked his possessions—women, children,
and slaves—with his name. In his naming powers and practices we see
the roots of the control Anne Jones describes when she says, "southern womanhood was born in the imaginations of white slaveholding
men" (8). In the following pages, however, we will look into the imaginations of two southern women, one white, one black, one named "lady,"
the other, "slave." We will see them actively, even if indirectly, practicing what Sandra Gilbert and Susan Gubar analyze as "strategies of
unnaming and renaming, strategies that directly address the problem of
woman's patronymically defined identity in western culture" (237). In
letters and autobiography, as they write the name of the man who was
their master, they effectively unname him. The patriarch, recreated in
their image and through their imagining, must answer to a new name.

My sources here are the writings of women who were, within the
patriarchal southern society they inhabited for a good portion of their
lives, silent beings; their writings thus bear an inevitable element of
secrecy. We often have to read between the lines. For Catherine Hammond's story, we must rely on her letters, few of which have been
published. Three of them appear in Carol Bleser's collection of three
generations of the Hammond family correspondence; the two letters that
I take as my text were written to her husband's brother, Marcus Hammond. The voice we hear in them is tentative, hesitant, careful. In order
to understand both what she says and what she does not say, we have to
fill in a great deal from research that has been conducted on Catherine's

husband, James Henry Hammond. For Harriet Jacobs's story, we can rely
on her autobiography, a book that represents a stunning act of breaking
silence, as this former slave took pen in hand during the turbulent decade of the 1850s to condemn what she bitterly called the "patriarchal
institution" (146) which still exercised great power over her life and the
lives of those she loved. Only recently, research by Jean Fagin Yellin
clearly established the fact that the voice we hear in this slave narrative
belongs to Harriet Jacobs. For far too long, historians easily acquiesced
to the notion that Jacobs's book, *Incidents in the Life of a Slave Girl*, had
been ghostwritten by her editor, Lydia Maria Child.[3] Now Jacobs's text
is a major resource for the study of black women's lives and strategies
for survival in slavery. Jacobs's best survival tool, as her narrative shows,
was her voice, her conception of the power of her own self-chosen words
wielded in the cause of freedom.

   The patriarchs whom these two women named and then redefined
through their writings were men well known and well established in
their communities. James Henry Hammond, a wealthy planter, governor,
senator, and staunch defender of South Carolina, was born the son of a
schoolmaster in the rural community of Mount Bethel, South Carolina,
in 1807.[4] Dr. James Norcom, born in 1778, practiced medicine in the
coastal town of Edenton, North Carolina, and owned close to two thousand acres of land in the surrounding county.[5] What we learn of these
prominent slaveholders from Catherine Hammond's and Harriet Jacobs's
writings is not what official records reveal, certainly not what these men
had to say for themselves. Indeed, we find that in Jacobs's narrative, Dr.
Norcom has lost even his name; in *Incidents,* she renames him Dr. Flint.
The Hammond letters and Jacobs narrative construct new images both
of the patriarch and the world that he ruled. Carol Christ writes that
"the simple act of telling a woman's story from a woman's point of view
is a revolutionary act. . . . Women writers who name the gap between
men's stories about women and women's own perceptions of self and
world are engaged in creating a new literary tradition" (7). Catherine
Hammond in her letters and Harriet Jacobs in her autobiography were
prophetically engaged in "naming the gap" between the master's definitions of wife and slave and their own visions of womanhood and slavery.
The revolutionary tradition which their writing reflects is a matriarchal

one, replacing the male concerns of caste and class with concern for the needs of children. Without question, race remained the strongest determinant of material condition. The code of patriarchal supremacy, however, determined for both the lady and the woman slave how they would be expected to use both their bodies and their minds. Seizing a voice, even indirectly, in such a society was indeed a revolutionary act.

The differences between Catherine Hammond and Harriet Jacobs are obvious enough. Born in 1814, Catherine Elizabeth Fitzsimons was, as historian Carol Bleser tells us, a "homely sixteen-year-old Charleston heiress" when James Henry Hammond began courting her in 1830 (4– 5). A year later they were married in a June wedding, but only after she had overcome the strenuous objections of her family. Because they rightly assumed that Hammond was more interested in the Fitzsimons name and wealth than in Catherine, they tried unsuccessfully to get him to renounce her dowry. Once married, Catherine satisfied her husband's dynastic ambitions in another manner besides her wealth: she bore five children in the first five years of their marriage. Harriet Jacobs, like Catherine Fitzsimons, found herself the object of a man's interest when she was sixteen, but for her there could be no June wedding. Harriet, as Yellin has determined through exhaustive research, was born in 1813, the daughter of slaves in Edenton, North Carolina. When she was sixteen, her master, Dr. Norcom, demanded that she become his concubine. To thwart him, she allowed the attentions of another prominent citizen of Edenton, Samuel Tredwell Sawyer. When Harriet became pregnant with Sawyer's child, her free grandmother first rebuked her but then provided shelter and some protection from Norcom's fury. Harriet bore two children by her white lover: a son, Joseph, in 1829, and a daughter, Louisa, in 1833. Catherine Hammond's children took, of course, their father's surname; Harriet Jacobs gave her children the surname of her own father, "who had himself no legal right to it," she explains, because "my grandfather on the paternal side was a white gentleman." She adds, "What tangled skeins are the genealogies of slavery!" (78).

In 1835, Harriet, fearing that the jealous Dr. Norcom would punish her for her "promiscuity" by placing her children with her on an outlying plantation, finally fled. What made her escape so unusual was that she did not leave the Edenton area but instead found refuge with women in her own community. First she hid with a black friend, then in the residence of a sympathetic white slaveholder, and finally in a hiding place designed by her relatives in her grandmother's home. What was meant to be a temporary shelter became a seven-years' residence; Harriet remained all those years in what she named her "loophole of retreat" while she waited to find some way to secure her children's safety. During the same years, Catherine Hammond bore more children—eight in all. In addition she managed domestic arrangements for her husband's estates, supporting him in his drive to become first a wealthy landowner, then a congressman, and finally governor of South Carolina.

In 1842, some time after her children were bought by their white father, Harriet Jacobs finally found means to make a successful escape to the North, where she could for the first time hope for her family's future. She found work as a housekeeper in the home of a prominent New York magazine editor, Nathaniel P. Willis. In 1850, when the passage of the Fugitive Slave Law made Harriet's situation more precarious, Cornelia Willis, always a sympathetic, generous employer, arranged to buy her freedom. Catherine Hammond's situation did not change so happily. In 1843, the Hammond family's fortunes took a decidedly downward turn. Catherine's deceased sister's husband, the powerful Wade Hampton, accused James Hammond of attempting to seduce his daughter, Catherine's niece. When the scandal was made public, Hammond's campaign for a seat in the United States Senate came to an abrupt end. Catherine stood by her husband even though she was sure to have suspected something of his goings-on, not just with one of her teenaged nieces, but with four of them. In his diary Hammond confessed that he had experienced "everything short of direct sexual intercourse" (Faust 242) with these girls. In 1850, however, Catherine was not so tolerant when she discovered her husband's sexual liaisons with two slaves, a mother and a daughter. Informing Hammond that she would not return until he had ended his affair with a slave named Louisa, Catherine left her husband. She did not reside permanently with him again until 1856.[6]

Both Catherine Hammond and Harriet Jacobs took desperate measures to escape what was, for each, an intolerable situation. Harriet's flight resulted in freedom and in the attainment of an increasingly active voice. In the early 1850s she began work on an autobiography that was published in 1861 under the pseudonym "Linda Brent." In these troubled years before the Civil War, while Harriet worked with other abolitionists and fugitives for an end to slavery, Catherine and James Hammond worked, after their reconciliation, to build a new plantation, Redcliffe, which became the family's permanent home. In 1858, Hammond's political prominence was restored when he was elected to the United States Senate, where, in a speech, he coined the phrase, "Cotton is King." The election of Lincoln, however, cut short his senatorial career. He returned to Redcliffe while his sons went off to fight for the Confederacy. According to his son Spann, Hammond willed his own death; shortly before he died on November 13, 1864, he predicted that the war would be over within six months and said, "I do not care to look beyond the veil" (Bleser 129).

After the war, Catherine Hammond was forced to sell much of her land, but she managed to retain Redcliffe and to aid her children in reestablishing their lives. For Harriet Jacobs, too, the Civil War changed life significantly. Using money from the sale of her autobiography, she returned to the South to aid the freedmen's cause. In 1867 she was able to visit the house which her grandmother had left to her in her will. Harriet Jacobs died in 1897; Catherine Hammond had died a year earlier. Harriet's daughter Louisa helped to organize meetings of the National Association of Colored Women during the 1890s, while Catherine's granddaughter Julia Bryan Hammond attended college at Harvard Annex and wrote, "By the side of my dear Grandmother's coffin, an inspiration came to me, a hope long mine became a conviction, humbly I dedicate my life to 'the struggle for others'" (Bleser 296). Daughter and granddaughter inherited, from the matriarchal side, not land or possessions but self-respect and a tradition of fighting for others as well as themselves.

What, then, did Catherine Hammond and Harriet Jacobs have in common? They were born one year apart, became the sexual interests of white men when they were the same age, bore children at close to the same time, and died a year apart. By birth and parentage, they belonged to the slaveholding South. Both came from loving families but were left fatherless at an early age. The chief difference, of course, was that Catherine Hammond inherited plantations and slaves from her father— and the freedom that came from having white parents. Harriet, on the other hand, inherited nothing from her father, and from her mother's "condition" as a slave she was bequeathed perpetual bondage. In spite of her status as a slave, however, she, like Catherine Hammond, asserted herself by insisting upon her right to choose the man with whom she would have sexual relations. And both women engaged in long battles with the men who had legal authority over them, one named husband, the other named master. The desire to shape their own fates was strong in both women, but the hope of doing so in a world where "master" meant white man was equally slim.

Harriet Jacobs chose to give herself to a man who could not "own" her except by her consent. Because that choice could not be ratified by marriage in her culture, she risked outraging her family's strong moral sense, to say nothing of the Victorian standards of the world that she would one day address as her readers. Hammond chose to give herself to a man who would "own" her from the moment of their marriage. And Carol Bleser says, "There is no evidence that [James Hammond] ever had pangs of conscience over his assumption that his wife and children were also a principal part of his possessions" (17). Was not the slave's act in this case an expression of freedom, while the lady's act was an acceptance of bondage? What we can glean from reading the Hammond letters and Jacobs's autobiography allows an especially ironic interpretation of the position of white and black southern women: Harriet Jacobs lived on the margins, with no protection of her womanhood or her motherhood, yet she freed herself—at huge costs, certainly. Catherine Hammond lived supposedly at the center of her culture's ideology, revered, protected, her roles as woman and mother exalted. Yet only the Civil War, which brought about her husband's fatalistic welcoming of death, freed this plantation mistress. The words of W. E. B. Du Bois come to mind here: "So some few women are born free, and some amid insult and scarlet letters achieve freedom; but our women in black had freedom thrust contemptuously upon them" (185). When we listen to the voices of Catherine Hammond and Harriet Jacobs, we hear differences in their degrees of freedom. Out of her marginality, Jacobs spoke her mind to an audience of sympathetic women that she in large measure shaped for herself, as we shall see; on her pedestal, Hammond found one sympathetic male relative to hear, first, her pleas for help and, finally, her declaration of independence.

Tillie Olsen writes of how "literary history and the present are dark with silences" (6). So too is the history of Catherine Hammond, wife of a man known, in spite of his blatant disregard for the humanity of those around him, as one of the Old South's most prominent intellectual and political leaders. And the dark silence of Catherine Hammond's story is, like the silences Olsen demarcates, "unnatural, the unnatural thwarting of what struggles to come into being, but cannot" (6). Only in the twilight of her life, as a widow, did Catherine Hammond find a voice. When we look at her three letters included in Carol Bleser's collection, *The Hammonds of Redcliffe,* what impresses most is what the letter-writer never says. In the last of the three, she writes to her son's mother-in-law to explain that she is moving out of Redcliffe so that her son and his family can have the home. "I but poorly express myself in writing" (170), she says simply. Her mistrust of her abilities with language might explain her silences, but the foundations of that mistrust were surely laid in her many years of submission to James Hammond's will. As we look at the two other letters in the Bleser collection, which Catherine wrote to her husband's brother, Marcus Hammond, we meet a woman for whom the act of deferring to male power was a part of her nature. Her father's death left her under the protection of her brothers; her marriage to Hammond gave him, in legal terms, complete control. When he died, Catherine, as we shall see, took the reins of her life, but ascribed the turn of events as God's will, not her own.[7] And while he lived, Hammond ruled; even though Catherine left him for almost five years, she returned and took up the role of silent giver that she had performed before.

Catherine Hammond's 1859 letter to Marcus Hammond is a study in tension. That she would write to him at all with the purpose of voicing personal family problems is somewhat unusual; her tone indicates that she knows the awkwardness of the situation. As we read some excerpts of her letter, written from Redcliffe on July 29, 1859, we can hear some striking alternations of tone, as need, duty, fear, love, and hostility compete for expression. One matter is settled: her husband's name is Father, and his authority is absolute.

My dear Brother:
    I read your letter to Mr. H. yesterday rec'd., I always read your letters, when he permits me to do so, with much interest and pleasure. You praise

the Genl., you urge most kindly the decisions of our boys and you admire Cattie—but you have for a long time entirely ignored me. Now as
I do not intend to be forgotten by one I so much esteem, I take the lib-
erty of presenting myself to you, and so, the necessary consequence of my
acquaintance, I come with a request. . . .

I cannot in a letter tell you all the little things which interfere with their
cooperating, and which I feel for the boys, I regret that they cannot overcome the difficulties, and entirely act in accordance with their Father's
wishes, which I have no doubt would be a great pecuniary advantage,
and give them for a few years the benefit of his experience. . . . And it
is not singular that men arriving at years of maturity—taking the heads
of their own families—should desire something independent and in their
own right. . . . I am myself utterly useless—helpless in my family—I don't
know how to advise the boys, and to open my mouth is only to bring a
storm on my own head that I often wish I could be dumb whenever the
subject is mentioned. . . . I can't help thinking tho' I fear to say what I
think best. I am very anxious about the boys. We have been quietly blessed
in this thus far and what is the use of all our means if it cannot bring us
peace. . . .

It seems an endless undertaking to bring things into order. . . . Mr. H. in
his frequent letters will give you all interesting information about himself.
I wish I could see him better satisfied and more at ease, and I tell him only
to decide on what he knows to be right and adhere to it, and there will not
be much difficulty in getting us all to approve. But what is the use of our
wanting things one way or another. We remain in his hands and we all feel
much more confidence in his decisions than in our own. I was at Mother's
last week she was cheerful and well except the heat which was very much
broken out on her. With love to Harriet and all.

I am yours very affectionately,
        C. E. H.

                                        (Bleser 69–71)

Catherine begins by almost coyly berating Marcus for neglecting her
—she is either whining or gently teasing at first, as she writes, "you
urge most kindly the decisions of our boys and you admire Cattie—
but you have for a long time entirely ignored me." Given the larger
context of surrounding correspondence in Bleser's collection, we can
assume that Marcus was singled out by Catherine largely because he
was a kindly, nonthreatening person who had sympathized before with

her sons' problems with James; like them, Marcus was a disappointment to his autocratic, perfectionist elder brother. Yet surely Catherine also turned to Marcus as her audience because, as a white male, he had at least some power. Her husband often consulted and confided in him, so Catherine could hope to use his influence with James. Speaking directly to her husband would not do. As she told Marcus, "to open my mouth is only to bring a storm on my own head that I often wish I could be dumb." Silence was her best protection.

The point of Catherine's letter is, not surprisingly, her children's needs and not her own. She writes Marcus to request his intercession on behalf of her sons at a time when James had threatened, evidently, to withdraw his financial support from them. The "boys," as she calls them, were grown, with families, and had been given homes and managerial positions on the Hammond plantations. Yet nothing they did ever suited James. He continually complained of their failures in farming his lands. In her letter, Catherine is eloquent in pleading her sons' case: "And it is not singular that men arriving at years of maturity—taking the heads of their own families—should desire something independent and in their own right." Yet a voice that is strong in understanding her children's need for independence becomes timid where the writer herself is concerned: "I can't help thinking tho' I fear to say what I think best"; "I am utterly useless"; "But what is the use of our wanting things one way or another." Only between the lines do we document her quiet desperation: "what is the use of all our means if it cannot bring us peace," she dares to ask. There is no question but that Catherine disagrees with her husband and thinks that his dictatorial ways are destroying her family, but she writes, "I tell him only to decide on what he knows to be right and adhere to it, and there will not be much difficulty in getting us all to approve." Her last words on the subject are chillingly fatalistic: "We remain in his hands." The purpose of the letter itself belies this assessment—Catherine does not give up on finding a way around her intransigent husband, yet indirection, behind-the-scenes manipulation, outward deference are her means. Hammond continued to rant about his sons' incompetence. In the end, the Civil War, not Marcus, intervened to decide the fates of all the Hammonds.

When Spann Hammond wrote to his brother Harry to tell him of his father's death, he also described his mother's reaction: "Mother simply exclaimed 'What! Dead? Dead?' but seemed incapable of realizing it" (Bleser 129). What were her emotions in that hour? We have to make our way through silence again to find a way to assess what the death of the master meant to the woman who was in many ways only his best slave. In a letter to Marcus Hammond written after the war had ended, with her children gathered around her, the Catherine Hammond who describes their situation speaks in a very different voice. She writes, again from Redcliffe, on September 3, 1865:

My dear Brother:

I was much gratified to receive your kind letter and Harriet's, and hear from you all. . . .

I cannot compare troubles and cares with you. I often can scarce restrain a burst of complaint at my change of circumstances—but as I compare my lot with many others, I see only cause for thankfulness. As to the future, if I could, I would scarce lift the curtain. We are in God's hands who alone has brought about this wonderful state of affairs and who only can unravel it. The boys are hopeful and very attentive to business. The crop promises well. We have not lost many negroes. I wish we could get rid of many of the useless ones. 300 mouths to feed is no small charge—meat and corn both low, but the new crop coming in. . . .

I hope you will save all Mr. Hammond's letters. . . . I can't trust myself with the past. Thank God I find more to do every day than I can accomplish and I am able to interest myself in it. My children are very kind and my household cheerful and satisfied. My servants behave pretty well. Robert has left. I have a very good boy to drive. The grounds around here are sadly neglected—but we keep but one man and there is too much. I do not know if I can keep this place—but enough trouble for the present —we need not anticipate. . . . I fear the work of the Convention touching Slavery—it is dead and I for one don't want it back. . . .

With love to all I am yours affectionately,

CEH

(Bleser 144–46)

Catherine Hammond's circumstances, as she says, are all changed, "but as I compare my lot with many others, I see only cause for thankfulness." The woman who had resigned her will to her husband's with the words "We remain in his hands" now says, "We are in God's hands who alone has brought about this wonderful state of affairs and who only can unravel it." She herself is not complaining about this change of governors. She mentions her son's plan to publish her husband's pamphlets, but adds, "I can't trust myself with the past." Her husband's name is, quite simply, no longer her concern. The pronoun "he," which dominated the earlier letter, has been replaced by "I" and "my." "Thank God," she exclaims, "I find more to do every day than I can accomplish and I am able to interest myself in it. My children are very kind and my household cheerful and satisfied. My servants behave pretty well." Contentment, assurance, authority shine through her claim to "my children," "my home," "my servants." God is in his heaven, "the boys are hopeful and very attentive to business," and "the crop promises well." It is September 3, 1865, the family is deeply in debt, the South has lost the war, but Catherine Hammond has won her household. Until her death in 1896, she stayed closely involved in her children's lives, evidently at their request. And in a final, ironic testimony, her sons named none of their sons after the father who had dreamed "of establishing a rich, educated, well-bred and prominent family . . . of our name" (Bleser 17). However, a granddaughter, Katharine Fitzsimons Hammond, attended Johns Hopkins Training School for Nurses and became the one whose son, John Shaw Billings, preserved and restored the family home of Redcliffe. Catherine's namesake granddaughter, and a matriarchal line, kept the ancestral Hammond dream alive.

Through the two letters of Catherine F. Hammond to Marcus Hammond, we witness an achievement of identity and voice defined in decisively woman's terms; her secure place as manager of her household and the respect of contented children provide Catherine Hammond's measure of herself. One of the quietly dramatic lessons that her letters teach concerns the effect of marriage on the woman of her time and class. Catherine Hammond changed from daughter-heiress to wife-mother, a predictable, almost inevitable transformation in the life of a southern girl of her class, one that she eagerly sought. Yet in truth her marriage guaranteed servitude and second-class status. As wife of James Hammond, she gave up her right to the inheritance left by her father along with her right to see herself as an independent human being for a state of permanent daughterhood, a patriarchally ordered dependency that lasted as long as her husband lived. Her life demonstrates what Bertram Wyatt-Brown calls "the curious but not unexpected fact that whereas woman's social existence depended upon her being married, her legal identity ended the moment the ceremony was performed" (254). Marriage meant social acceptance; it also meant bondage. Catherine Hammond's struggle to express herself within boundaries that she did not dare to confront directly is a story with many gaps, many silences. Only death and the changes wrought by a devastating war took away her husband's claim to her voice. Once freed, she raised it to celebrate quietly her discovery that she could transform his name and his house into her own.

The ideology that determined Catherine Hammond's lack of identity has been defined by Nina Baym as a "simple" one which decreed that "woman was naturally designed for the home and the private sphere; laws aiming to keep her there were for her own benefit as well as the public good; women who felt legally or culturally restrained were unnatural; women who, for whatever reason, had to leave the home were pitiable and of no account" (212). Catherine Hammond's letters reveal, though only sketchily, one side of the effects of this ideology. Another side is probed in much fuller detail and in a far clearer voice by Harriet Jacobs, whose vantage point on the ideology was determined for her by her total exclusion from it. A slave woman, as James Henry Hammond's story and Harriet Jacobs's both show, was not "naturally designed for the home." She was designed instead for her master's pleasure, whatever that happened to be. In James Hammond's letters and plantation records we see that his slave concubine, Louisa, was moved around continually as he sought ways to circumvent his wife's demands that she be sold. Likewise, Harriet Jacobs, as a woman slave, could have no home; her owner was actually cruelly reminding her of this fact when he promised her, in return for compliance with his sexual demands, that he would give her a "home of [her] own and make a lady of [her]" (53). As we witness how Dr. Norcom (renamed Flint) couches his plan to make Jacobs a prostitute in the pious, sentimental language of true womanhood, we are able to gauge the potential for hypocrisy underlying the ideology which Baym describes.

When Jacobs announced, at the close of her narrative, "Reader, my story ends with freedom; not, in the usual way, with marriage" (201), she

was not only revising the traditional finale that her culture prescribed
for a woman's story, she was also envisioning her own creation. Her next
sentence, "I and my children are now free!" declared her creative powers
as mother and head of her family. Behind this empowerment is a transformation even more dramatic and ironic than Catherine Hammond's,
because Jacobs achieved her voice from within her culture's darkest cage.
Historically, she was not only woman, but black slave woman, with three
decrees of speechlessness and dependency governing her existence. Yet
she dared to tell her story, with the clear purpose of reversing the effects
of a soul-killing patriarchal institution upon her goal of selfhood. More
than that, she appropriated the patriarch's function—creator, designer,
builder—within the act of writing, and by that means turned the structure of patriarchy against itself. The focus of her story, from the title
to the last paragraph, is her role as shaper of her life; the plot is her
struggle against conditions of race, gender, and region which combined
to keep her from owning her life; the characters are all agents or objects
of change. In the two main characters, herself (renamed Linda Brent)
and Norcom (renamed Dr. Flint), she creates a slave woman who defied
all of the conventions that combined to make her the victim and a male
slaveholder who lost his power to control when his words, in the mouth
of his slave, became her best weapon against him. As we look at the title
and the plot of her book, we are looking at a woman writer who created
her identity as woman and writer when she found the voice with which
to tell her story.

The title *Incidents in the Life of a Slave Girl: Written by Herself* is
rich in contradictions which predict the struggles to come. First, this
is not a "life," but "incidents" from a life. Jacobs as slave author insists
upon what most of the slave narrators tried to downplay: her role as
selector and shaper of her story. The slave narrative as an abolitionist
text had to meet special demands of "truth"; thus editors and narrators alike stressed the "unvarnished" nature of the eyewitness accounts
of life under slavery.[8] Jacobs's title-word, "incidents," declares a process
through which the writer chooses how she wants her life to look, an
honest but daring position to voice. A second collision occurs in the title
when "life" is qualified by "slave girl." What could be the "life" of one
who, by law, could know herself and be known only as "slave" and "girl,"

labels which inscribed the bearer as doubly a nonentity. And Jacobs sets up a third conflict with the addition of the obligatory phrase, "written by herself." These words authenticated virtually every slave narrative title, indicating again abolitionist editors' concern that the slaves' accounts be accepted as trustworthy. The fact that the phrase was appended to Jacobs's narrative attests to the presence of editors, skeptical readers, a hostile southern press—a host of forces attempting to dictate the shape and function of the story that followed. Furthermore, for a so-called "girl" to write, particularly about her "self," was, while not impossible, hardly commendable in the era of "true womanhood." For this female slave, then, to write her own book and to proclaim that act was both a sacrifice to convention that might compromise the freedom of the text and a challenge to patriarchal prescriptions against women's or slaves' rights to a voice.

With its many conflicting elements, Jacobs's title attests to both her struggle and her determination. Her choice of an epigraph from Isaiah 22:9 asserts her will to subvert patriarchy by authorizing herself as the creative force both outside and within the text. With Isaiah's language she identifies a specific audience and a bold conception of authorial voice: "Rise up, ye women that are at ease! Hear my voice, ye careless daughters! Give ear unto my speech." Through the prophet's exhortation, Jacobs appropriates a call to heroic womanhood that counters the label of anonymous "girl"; moreover, she claims a gift of superior knowledge before "careless daughters" and announces possession of a rallying voice. In her preface, Jacobs indicates that she found the courage to publish her account out of a sense of belonging to the community of women that the words of Isaiah invoke. Her goal was, she says, to "arouse the women of the North to a realizing sense of the condition of two millions of women at the South, still in bondage, suffering what I suffered, and most of them far worse" (1). In shaping her book, Jacobs simultaneously defined and relied upon this sense of two communities—one free in the North and one in bondage in the South—yet both bearing the burden of patriarchally imposed silence.

Jacobs's title page and preface indicate the plot's arrangement into a confrontation between opposing forces. However, freedom vs. bondage, North vs. South, male vs. female forms of knowledge and power, girl-

hood vs. womanhood, speech vs. silence, are not abstract concepts but
concrete conditions of the writer's life through which she moves and
which she finally harnesses to her own purposes. The first sentence of
her narrative shows Jacobs defining her life in terms of divisions that
are her means, ultimately, of reordering perception. She writes, "I was
born a slave; but I never knew it till six years of happy childhood had
passed away" (5). In an opening that was traditional for slave narratives
as indeed for all autobiography, Jacobs announces, "I was born," yet the
second part of her sentence shrewdly calls the nature of that existence
into question. Her strategy reflects a conflict which all of the more carefully designed slave narratives arranged between two versions of reality
—to be born a slave yet to refuse to know oneself as a slave is to set
up opposing orders and levels of both being and knowing. As a child
Jacobs was kept from being a slave only by her happy ignorance. Later
she would need to enact a different order of being out of full knowledge
of her culture's proscriptive image of her. This becomes the plot of her
divided text.

In analyzing the place of plot in shaping a feminist poetics of the
novel, Joanne Frye says that "every narrative is based on a choice of
which information is relevant and which irrelevant" (38). As we have
noted, the word "incidents" in her title indicates Jacobs's understanding
of her narrative as a way both to achieve and to exhibit the power connected to freedom of choice. The writer who makes self the subject of
her book shapes her life as she decides sequence, transitions, and metaphors. At one point in her narrative, as Jacobs tells her readers how the
white community of Edenton responded to the 1831 Nat Turner rebellion, she focuses on a group of illiterate "poor whites" who entered her
grandmother's attractive, well-ordered little home. In preparation for the
"country bullies," she says, she and her grandmother "arranged every
thing in my grandmother's house as neatly as possible," for she knew that
"nothing annoyed them so much as to see colored people living in comfort and respectability" (63). As the mob searched through fine linen,
exclaiming over silver spoons and dainty jars of preserves, Jacobs and
her grandmother stood aside, offering in their dignity, cold composure,
and use of proper English a complete contrast to the white men who are
shown to be only brutes, and powerless, frustrated brutes at that. In the

process of selecting and shaping this minor incident, Jacobs the writer organizes and interprets the world according to her own controlling vision. The womanly art of housekeeping becomes a metaphor of her strategy as a writer, a designing woman skilled at "arranging everything . . . neatly."

Throughout her story Jacobs shows herself in the act of choosing while she also shows her master as manipulated by her choices, frustrated in his attempt to carry out his own designs, and reacting to her decisions instead of acting on his own. Jacobs makes the situation, the setting, and the characters of her narrative function as metaphors of her empowerment. When I use the word "metaphor" here, I am drawing upon James Olney's definition of the word as the dominant trope of autobiography: metaphors are "all the world views and world pictures, models and hypotheses, myths and cosmologies, . . . something known and of our making, or at least of our choosing, that we put to stand for, and so to help us understand, something unknown and not of our making; they are that by which consciousness gives order not only to itself but to as much of objective reality as it is capable of formalizing and controlling" (*Metaphors of Self* 30). Implicit in Olney's analysis of how the autobiographical imagination functions is the assertion of power, and particularly the power of self-creation, involved in invoking metaphoric dimensions of experience. As the self "expresses itself by the metaphors it creates," it gives order, formalizes, controls. A brief examination of two places in Jacobs's narrative where she emphasizes herself as agent in acts of unconventional choice-making will indicate how she saw herself as Olney's type of "shape-maker" (17, 18). In these scenes, Jacobs accomplishes several goals: she overturns plot expectations decreed by a male-organized value system; she redefines the basis of power so that women's modes of control become dominant; and she supplants the South's controlling patriarchal mythology with a new myth governed by metaphoric figures of a matriarch and an effective, racially diverse community of women.

Perhaps the most dramatic instance in which Jacobs projects herself as "shape-maker" involves her master's scheme to build a cabin outside of town where she would live as his concubine. The language that Dr. Flint uses in making this proposition is borrowed from the promise-of-home rhetoric abounding in women's plots of the mass-market literature of the 1850s. "I was constrained to listen," Jacobs says, "while he talked of his intention to give me a home of my own, and to make a lady of me" (53). Dr. Flint blatantly rewrites his culture's dream of the pure, protected lady for his own polluted ends. More importantly, however, Jacobs, by her careful shaping of his language in her summary, allows his words to indict him. Her reaction to his proposal emphasizes her image of herself not as victim (the conventional characterization of the damsel whose virtue is threatened by the rake) but as powerful adversary: "I would do any thing," she vows, "every thing, for the sake of defeating him. What *could* I do?" She immediately answers her question with a radical plan: she willfully allows the advances of "a white unmarried gentleman" who around this time became "interested" in her (54).

Jacobs explains at length her reasons for forming a sexual liaison with Samuel Tredwell Sawyer, renamed Mr. Sands in her narrative. Part of her motivation was surely her need to reassure her white, genteel, and primarily female readers concerning her qualifications as accuser and judge of southern slaveholders. As the unmarried mother of two children, she would have much explaining to do if she expected readers to accept her moral vision. Jacobs, however, undercuts this motivation. She does say, "I know I did wrong. . . . The painful and humiliating memory will haunt me to my dying day" (55–56). Yet as she tells what went through her mind when she accepted Sands's attentions, she clearly asserts her need and her right to make this revolutionary decision. She also makes a clear distinction between the victimized teenager who was forced to act and the mature writer who is recreating the event in her story. "Still, in looking back, calmly, on the events of my life," the writer tells us, "I feel that the slave woman ought not to be judged by the same standards as others" (56). The male double standard is here reversed with a vengeance.

Jacobs's first explanation of her choice of Mr. Sands involves self-respect. And self-respect was not, given her gender or her race, a luxury that her culture allowed her. Catherine Hammond, we remember, was totally silent concerning her right as a wife and mother to contribute even to basic family decisions. Jacobs, on the other hand, breaks silence on an especially delicate issue in a voice that asserts her rights simply as a woman: "It seems less degrading to give one's self, than to submit to compulsion. There is something akin to freedom in having a lover who has no control over you, except that which he gains by kindness and attachment" (55). Jacobs's second explanation of her choice is in some ways even more shocking: "Revenge, and calculations of interest, were added to flattered vanity and sincere gratitude for kindness" (55), she confesses. As she calculated her master's response to discovering that she favored another, Jacobs could even boast that "it was something to triumph over my tyrant even in that small way" (55). Added to the decidedly unwomanly motivation of revenge was her speculation that, if she were to have children by her master, he would surely sell them; however, if she bore another man's children, her master might be angry enough to sell her and the children to friends who could secure their freedom. To consciously attempt to manipulate child-bearing capacities for her own ends was a power play taken from the patriarch's own book. In no way does Jacobs rewrite her culture's plot more radically than when she not only asserts the prerogative of choosing her sexual part-ner but admits to carefully calculated self-interest as the reason for her choice.

We need to pay particular attention, in reviewing Jacobs's words here, to what the writer accomplishes as she tells her reader of her thoughts. Later events would show that she miscalculated. Dr. Flint was deter-mined to see his slave suffer for spurning him and to show her that he could control her life in at least some essential respects. But as she gives her rationale to her readers, accounting for what actually took place later matters far less than demonstrating that she can fight, that she has no in-tention of being victimized, and that what happened to her was a result of her very conscious decision-making. The whole scene thus overturns what we expect from Flint's opening proposition. This writer knows her culture's standard plot resolution for her situation, and she wants her reader to understand that her role is not to submit to but to revise that story. Thus she transforms the damsel in distress into a powerful agent for change and the patriarch into a powerless cuckold.

A second instance of the writer as selector and shape-maker through metaphor concerns Jacobs's dramatization of how she existed in her grandmother's tiny garret, "nine feet long and seven wide," during the seven years that she hid from Dr. Flint a block away from his own home. Jacobs's description of this cramped, closed-in space comes in chapter 21 of her forty-one chapter narrative—at the center, then, of the life that she arranged in her book. She gives this space a metaphoric dimension even in the chapter title, for she calls it her "loophole of retreat," a reference to lines from William Cowper's "The Task."[9] Here, at the midway point of her narrative, Jacobs sets up this home within a home, a kind of still center hidden in the midst of the turbulence, even frenzy, of the master's domain. While physically immobilized in her hiding place, Jacobs still was able to transform the room that she called a cage into a theatre. Almost her first act in her garret prison was to bore an inch-square hole in the wall so that she could look out on the street below. This small peephole allowed her to see and to frame the outside world. Again, I emphasize here what Jacobs the writer is doing in this scene: she is self-consciously using the materials of her situation to construct a vision of herself as shaper. Unable to move or to speak, she makes the whole world, as it were, parade by her tiny window. She reports overhearing conversations that make her the subject of an important community drama; she describes her master's furious comings and goings, making it seem as though she is at the center of his every move; she shows herself bearing witness, with the slaveholding world as her stage. As she compares the safety of her "retreat," however circumscribed, to the evil taking place in the streets below, Jacobs reinforces her claim to a superior power strategy that women could call upon precisely because of their ability to control interior space.

Two activities—observing and writing—counteracted the effects of silence, secrecy, and darkness that Jacobs's hideout symbolized. From a kind of "world within," she shows herself emerging not only as seer but also as author. Telling of a trick that she designed for Dr. Flint, she presents an image of herself writing as well as witnessing in a way that makes her the creator, arranger, and speaker of her own version of events. While in hiding, Jacobs read newspapers from New York, which she turned into her own proofs. From them she gathered dates and street names which she attached to fake letters to her grandmother and Dr. Flint. The letters described her fictitious new life as a free woman living in the North. A friend took the letters with him to New York and mailed them back to Edenton. Dr. Flint somehow received both his own and the grandmother's letters; when he went to the grandmother's house to read "Linda's" letter to her, Jacobs eavesdropped while he substituted his own words for the ones she actually wrote in her fabricated story. "This was as good as a comedy to me," she says (130). Assuming his slave to be in the North, Dr. Flint stopped searching for her in Edenton. Listening a few yards above him, she could manipulate her master and expose his theft of her voice.

In the later chapters of her narrative, dealing with her life after her escape, Jacobs writes Dr. Flint out of the plot completely. With him goes the whole structure of patriarchal influence. Another way that she handles the transformation of the father's stronghold into the mother's domain is her description of the father-daughter relationship between her lover and her daughter Louisa. Mr. Sands had purchased Jacobs's children but had never freed them. While serving as a congressman in Washington, D.C., he let his slave daughter act as servant to his white daughter, then "gave" her to a niece living in Brooklyn. When Jacobs finally found Louisa and arranged for her freedom, she decided to confess the nature of her relationship with Sands. Her daughter's reply overturns the structure of the father-based family, a revision necessitated by the abuses of the patriarchal system. Louisa says, "I know all about it, mother. . . . I am nothing to my father, and he is nothing to me" (189). Explaining how Sands never acknowledged her as his daughter, she continues, "I thought if he was my own father, he ought to love me. I was a little girl then, and didn't know any better. But now I never think any thing about my father. All my love is for you." The mother-daughter kinship becomes the sustaining human bond here, as it was in the relationship between Jacobs and her grandmother. Jacobs ends her book by calling up "tender memories of my good old grandmother" (201). As she looks forward to life in freedom with her daughter, she also looks back to a figure who is, for the antebellum slave narrative genre as a whole, a unique metaphor of a successfully organized matriarchy—continually threatened, yet never defeated. Grandmother Marthy does more than just endure—she owns her home, a center of women's activities that can only be termed revolutionary.

Incidents in the Life of a Slave Girl does not move toward an altogether happy ending, for Jacobs reminds her reader that she herself still has no home. "The dream of my life is not yet realized," she says. "I do not sit with my children in a home of my own. I still long for a hearth-stone of my own, however humble. I wish it for my children's sake far more than for my own" (201). If we count the repetitions of the word "my" that occur in this passage—"my life," "my home," "my children," "my own"—we see that Jacobs holds up the idea of self-ownership, a vision that she kept steadily before her from the time she recognized, as a fifteen-year-old, that Dr. Flint's claim to her represented nothing less than self-annihilation. The vision at the end of *Incidents* is not complete; full justification still lies ahead.

A different finale for Jacobs's story exists in a letter that she wrote to her friend Ednah Dow Cheney after the war. Finally, in 1867, she, like Catherine Hammond, was able to take possession of her home. Molly Horniblow willed the house she owned in Edenton to her granddaughter, Harriet Jacobs. On April 25, 1867, Jacobs described in her letter what it meant to sit "under the old roof twelve feet from the spot where I suffered all the crushing weight of slavery" (249). She found that her attachment to "my old home" came in the form of memories of the people there whom she had loved, an attachment, then, based not on ownership of property but on shared experience, mutual pain, "unfaltering love." What she recognized, too, was that by 1867, "The change is so great I can hardly take it all in." In her book, she spoke into being a new identity based on roles she chose for herself—mother, nurturer, teacher, home-maker. In her letter, the words "my old home" finalize her appropriation of a completed self. These words link her again to Catherine Hammond, writing an identity for herself as she reports, "My children are very kind and my household cheerful and satisfied" (Bleser 145). Here were two women who could say in one breath that slavery "is dead and I for one don't want it back." As with slavery, so with the patriarchs who had governed their lives. In letters and in autobiography, Catherine Hammond and Harriet Jacobs began the process of unnaming and unraveling the tight skein of white southern male influence. To her letters, Catherine Hammond signed her name. For her autobiography, Harriet Jacobs created a new name. Both women thus testified in their own voices to the end of woman's silence and to the beginning of a powerful tradition of creative woman's voice.

CHAPTER TWO

Prodigal Daughters

The Journeys of Ellen Glasgow, Zora Neale Hurston, and Eudora Welty

The stories of Catherine Hammond and Harriet Jacobs teach us that the road home often begins as a road away from home. These were women who defined themselves in terms of their connections with others and who then experienced unsettling, threatening disruptions which sparked quests for new self-definitions. And when both the plantation lady and the slave found ways to fashion separate, individual voices, they were able to reestablish their homes, as they had established themselves, upon new grounds. Quests for voice led Catherine Hammond and Harriet Jacobs to language: as they wrote down their stories, language led them away from the patriarch's home, toward themselves. Thus we can view the act of writing as an act of separation, an act of leaving home. For Hammond and Jacobs, to break silence was to break away from home. The act of seizing a voice for self-expression separated them from the patriarchs, whom they redefined in appropriating language to explain themselves. Words separated, but words also forged new bonds; writing became a way of bonding, a way not just of knowing themselves but of redefining relationships with others. Naming the patriarch first freed these writers from him; then the naming, and in particular Jacobs's use of metaphor to rename, gave each woman knowledge of and thereby control over her field of vision. Catherine Hammond and Harriet Jacobs chose to know, and thus to be connected to, home and family, yet they were able to insist, through their mastery of language, on their power to name the terms of their homecoming.

The process that I have been describing for the plantation wife and the fugitive slave woman is, in many ways, an imaginative reconstruction of their psychological journey. It is a process that, for the most part, we have to infer. Catherine Hammond's two brief letters and Harriet Jacobs's publicly shaped and directed autobiography do not announce explicitly the inward journey that I have projected for them. In this chapter we turn to women for whom writing also became both a separating and a connecting act, a way of both leaving and returning home. In reviewing the autobiographies of Ellen Glasgow, Zora Neale Hurston, and Eudora Welty, we will be able to make more definite assertions about the inward nature of the daughter's relationship to home and the southern woman's relationship to her culture. Glasgow, Hurston, and Welty shaped their autobiographies to trace the routes that took them away from and back to their fathers' houses. Thus I have named them "prodigal daughters," not so much to equate their stories with the biblical parable as to emphasize their transformation of it. Their homecomings are marked not with repentance nor with a request to return to the old order, but with the assertion of achievements that rewrite patriarchal definitions of both home and daughter.

In *The Woman Within*, Ellen Glasgow tells a story which helps to explain what the term "prodigal daughter" would have meant to the South of the early twentieth century. Her father, Francis Glasgow, a stern and unsentimental businessman, loved reading sentimental novels. His daughter relates how, as he read one of these works made for "easy tears," "his voice would quiver and break, and tears would overflow his eyes, whenever he encountered in print the return of a prodigal daughter. Oddly enough, the prodigal son left him untouched, at least to all outward signs" (86). In western culture generally, the prodigal son's path away from home has always been accepted as an essential direction. Who would want to be the son who stayed home? Who expects the son to stay home? The prodigal son is a hero, in his leaving as well as in his return. Joseph Campbell explains that it is with "the passing over a boundary" that "the adventure begins. . . . You can't have creativity unless you leave behind the bounded, the fixed, all the rules" (156). So the son who strays in the biblical story enacts a standard heroic myth—for males. When asked if the heroes of the different mythic traditions were required to be men, Campbell responded, "Oh no. The male usually has the more conspicuous role, just because of the conditions of life. He is out there in the world, and the woman is in the home" (125). A woman's "heroism," then, is confined in myth to bearing and raising children. For her to wander, to take the journey into creativity that Campbell associates with adventures beyond "the bounded, the fixed" rules of home, is scarcely conceivable. Certainly the sight of the penitent daughter returning to her expected role would bring tears to the eyes of a father, especially one like Francis Glasgow, who organized his household on a strictly patriarchal model.

The idea of the prodigal daughter works for me as a metaphor to emphasize the difference between the male and female versions of heroism that southern communities accepted, but even more importantly as a metaphor to characterize the kind of autobiographies that the women writers of this chapter designed. Glasgow, Hurston, and Welty journeyed away from home and then returned, not in order to reconstruct the world they had left but to see it and create it anew from changed angles of vision. Glasgow began writing *The Woman Within* in 1934, when she was around sixty. She finished her work on the book some time near her death in 1945, but it was not published until 1954. Hurston wrote her autobiography, *Dust Tracks on a Road,* in the summer of 1941, when she was probably around fifty years old, and published it the following year.[1] *One Writer's Beginnings* began as the William E. Massey, Sr., Lectures at Harvard University, which Welty delivered in 1983, when she was seventy-four. All three autobiographies are thus "late" works that followed the years of their authors' greatest creative output as fiction writers. All three were conceived and enacted as a means to explore, as well as to complete, the writer's definition of herself as writer. Glasgow intended her title to describe her idea of authorship, for elsewhere she wrote that "the natural writer must, of necessity, live on the surface the life of accepted facts, which is the life of actions and shadows, while with his deeper consciousness he continues to live that strangely valid life of the mind" (*CM* vii). The "dust tracks" on Hurston's road were the words that gave meaning to her wandering. Welty's beginnings, as her title claims, were a writer's beginnings. In this chapter, I will first define the kind of autobiographies that resulted from these women's sense of their works as writers' homeward journeys. Then I will explore the three similar territories through which their travels took them: the territory of home, the territory of the journey within, and the territory of return.

Autobiographers of Memory

Glasgow, Hurston, and Welty establish in their autobiographies a connection between remembering and creating that allows us to call them "autobiographers of memory," a term James Olney adopts for writers who employ memory in a "creative sense." All three women engage in the process he describes when he theorizes that "time carries us away from all of our earlier states of being: memory recalls those earlier states—but it does so only as a function of present consciousness." The importance of the autobiographical act for a writer who depends on memory in this way lies in its creative power: Olney says it "shapes and reshapes the historic past in the image of the present, making that past as necessary to this present as this present is the inevitable outcome of that past" ("Versions" 243). Glasgow, Hurston, and Welty return through memory to their daughterhood homes but assess those homes with writers' eyes. The voices that call back the past belong to women who are far removed, in knowledge as well as time, from the selves formed by and within home and family. The act of remembering alters both the images of the past and the autobiographer's construction of herself in the present.

When Eudora Welty describes, in *One Writer's Beginnings,* what she learned from looking at her past, she confirms Olney's theory of the "autobiography of memory." She tells us that "through learning at my later date things I hadn't known, or had escaped or possibly feared realizing, about my parents—and myself—I glimpse our whole family life as if it were freed of that clock time which spaces us apart so inhibitingly, divides young and old, keeps our living through the same experiences at separate distances" (102). Here knowledge, fear, escape, and freedom join to make Welty's enterprise clearly a heroic one. What she describes as "our inward journey that leads us through time—forward or back, seldom in a straight line," is the direction that memory makes possible.

Creative transformation, the hero's right, results: "as we discover, we remember," she says, and "remembering, we discover" (102). Glasgow, too, had a sense of how homecoming, or past-finding, unlocks meanings for the present. In *The Woman Within* she enters her scene to say, "I am recording these episodes chiefly in the endeavor to attain a clearer understanding of my own dubious identity and of the confused external world in which I have lived" (130). Zora Neale Hurston voices a similar awareness of the two-directional nature of the autobiographical quest. She comments in *Dust Tracks* that "I did not know then, as I know now, that people are prone to build a statue of the kind of person that it pleases them to be. And few people want to be forced to ask themselves, 'What if there is no me like my statue?'" (34). Glasgow, Hurston, and Welty returned home in autobiography to ask this question, to bring the remembering self and all the statues of the past together in affirmation of the "me" whom they discovered.

The conception that connects all of the selves that meet in these three autobiographies is, as we have seen, the author's sense of her identity as writer. Each work contains a scene designed to show that words and stories enacted the child's sense of self and gave her the means through which she could make the world in her image. Glasgow gives perhaps the most dramatic expression of this early commitment to the writer's identity in *The Woman Within* as she says, "Below the animated surface, I was already immersed in some dark stream of identity, stronger and deeper and more relentless than the external movement of living. It was not that I had so early found my vocation. At the age of seven my vocation had found me. The one permanent interest, the single core of unity at the center of my nature, was beginning to shape itself, and to harden. I was born a novelist, though I formed myself into an artist" (41). Glasgow's lifelong journey is marked out in this statement, a journey that moved her inward to a centered self and then outward to an artist's confirmation of that self.

Hurston, like Glasgow, found within herself a "single core of unity" when, as a child, she discovered her affinity for storytelling. In *Dust Tracks,* she connects this center with the heart of her community, the store porch of Eatonville where the men gathered to tell stories. Of course "I was not allowed to sit around there" (62), Hurston says. Nonetheless her autobiography testifies to her successful appropriation of this man's place, source of a traditionally male power—the power of language itself. Hurston, even as a child, grasped the nature of this power in a way that set her apart from her community. In *Dust Tracks* she explains, "No doubt, these tales of God, the Devil, animals and natural elements seemed ordinary enough to most people in the village. But many of them stirred up fancies in me. It did not surprise me at all to hear that animals talked. I had suspected it all along. Or let us say, that I wanted to suspect it. Life took on a bigger perimeter by expanding on these things. I picked up glints and gleams out of what I heard and stored it away to turn it to my own uses" (69). Hurston's play on the word "store" demonstrates how she gave herself permission to sit where stories were made and to surprise the world with her own talk.

Welty, too, discovered as a child the dark, in some ways forbidden, yet also magical stream of identity that the others recognized in the writer's vocation. She describes how, at the age of six, she became physically aware of the word: "The word 'moon' came into my mouth as though fed to me out of a silver spoon. Held in my mouth the moon became a word" (10). The child who in this moment discovers the power of language creates the moon with all of its connections to woman's life, woman's rhythms, woman's knowledge. In all three scenes, images— a dark stream, a store, a silver spoon—connect the woman writer to the child beginning her creative, heroic transformation. Discovery and memory combine as the artist voices the realization that she has created a world in the act of choosing her image.

Glasgow, Hurston, and Welty designed their autobiographies to be quests for, as well as proof of, the writer's identity. Words and stories, as their early visions recorded, were to be the means by which their lives took shape. Other methods of achieving form, for either their lives or their autobiographies, were secondary. In organizing events for their autobiographies, each writer arranged a series of selected scenes and experiences that might be said to constitute her "life," in a chronological sense; however, the direction that resulted was hardly a straight or forward one.[2] Chapters or sections that seem to be divided according to time sequence or subject matter do not follow these divisions at all—all three autobiographers jump ahead or return to earlier territory in their narratives with little concern for chronological direction or continuity of subject. Glasgow announces at one point that her memory had "a firm, wide-reaching power to retain the words and rhythms of poetry, as well as all visual impressions, scenes, colors, and scents," yet it "has always been, and is now, incapable of permanently recording a date or a number" (77). "Pictures," she adds, "are indelible, but figures are immediately washed from the slate of my recollection." With this perception Glasgow exempts herself from the kind of order that one might expect from autobiography, an ordering, we can add, that she associated with her father. Hurston and Welty, too, defined time and rational, sequential ordering as fathers' preoccupations. Like Glasgow, they reconstructed events within pictorial frames rather than along chronological lines.

Glasgow indicated another aspect of her autobiography's form when she wrote to her literary executors describing *The Woman Within:* "I was writing for my own release of mind and heart; and I have tried to make a completely honest portrayal of an interior world, and of that one world alone" (v). *The Woman Within, Dust Tracks on a Road,* and *One Writer's Beginnings* all portray interior worlds that are, as Welty said, free of clock time. The sections of Glasgow's and Hurston's stories that deal with their lives through girlhood and the whole of Welty's autobiography achieve form from pictures that the writer draws and from the consistency of the voice that makes the frames. Both Glasgow and Hurston speak more pictorially in the earlier chapters of their autobiographies, when they describe childhood selves in the process of attaining voices and visions; when they reach periods where their "lives" became more officially known, the events, and the voices that convey them, lose some of their poetry. The interior childhood world, closely connected to home, is a reservoir of metaphors for the writer intent on finding and expressing self. The early sections of both *The Woman Within* and *Dust Tracks* are unified by the writer's poetically imaged quest for self and by her strategy, the double focus of memory and discovery. I will emphasize these sections in relation to Welty's *One Writer's Beginnings.* Welty's three-part structure separates "Listening" in part 1 from "Learning to See" and "Finding a Voice" in the latter two sections. Yet in all three parts, a childhood self coexists with an adult writer who exults in the capacities that language gives her for bringing memory to bear on experience and experience to bear on memory. Perhaps because her book originated as lectures, Welty's soft, questioning, Mississippi voice permeates the whole and gives *One Writer's Beginnings* throughout the tone of a quest. Her patterns of listening and learning at home, then seeking and finding a voice through which to leave and return home, provide the direction that we will attempt to follow in all three works.

Living at Home: The Daughter's Vision

Home for most of Ellen Glasgow's life was One West Main Street in Richmond, Virginia. Glasgow takes us to this central place in her life in chapter 3 of *The Woman Within:* "When I was very small, my father bought a farm, and, a little later, he sold the old house on Cary Street, and moved his family into a still older and larger house on the corner of Foushee and Main Streets. This is the square gray house where I have lived for the rest of my life, and where I have written all my books, with the exception of *Life and Gabriella*" (26). Glasgow lived, then, in her father's house for almost her entire life. During childhood, the house was controlled by the presence of this patriarchal figure who could "move his family" wherever he chose. Before we actually meet the father or see this house, his controlling presence is introduced in the autobiography's first image. Glasgow opens her autobiography with a glimpse of the woman's consciousness within the infant that she imagines herself to be. This consciousness records the infant's world of pure sensation: "I see the firelight, but I do not know it is firelight. I hear singing, but I do not recognize my mother's voice" (3). Clearly, Glasgow is reconstructing how she felt in the security of her mother's world, "rocked in my mother's arms" at a time when "I do not know that I am myself." This world of gratified feelings, where mother and daughter exist in undifferentiated peace, is threatened by a terrifying force which represents both male power and consciousness itself. She relates that suddenly "I see a face without a body staring in at me, a vacant face, round, pallid, grotesque, malevolent. . . . One minute, I was not; the next minute, I was. I felt. I was separate. I could be hurt" (3–4). Throughout the childhood sections of *The Woman Within,* Glasgow associates her father with separations from her mother, with malevolence, yet also with language and with the consciousness that gave her the will to survive and to write.

Glasgow's home is divided by her conflicting responses to her parents. Hatred for the father begins with the image of the face that "stabbed" her into consciousness. On the other hand, her mother was "the center of my childhood," the one with whom Glasgow associates tenderness and encouragement. Anne Gholson Glasgow was an Anglican Tidewater-Virginia belle who "made everything luminous" and whose "whole nature was interwoven with sympathy" (13–14). Francis Glasgow, his daughter says quite bluntly, "was one of the last men on earth that she should have married" (14). Francis Glasgow hailed from the western regions of Virginia but moved to Richmond to manage his uncle's ironworks. In religion as in regional orientation and class, he differed completely from his wife. The father was "stalwart, unbending, rock-ribbed with Calvinism," an upright but sour man who "never committed a pleasure" (15). Father becomes other, an alien, all-powerful, masculine presence who separates his daughter from her mother's nurturing presence. In the autobiography, Glasgow retaliates by erasing her father's imprint with these scathingly ironic words: "but we were made of different clay, and I inherited nothing from him, except the color of my eyes and a share in a trust fund, which he had accumulated with infinite self-sacrifice. Everything in me, mental or physical, I owe to my mother" (16).

Glasgow's hostility toward her father owed a great deal to what she doubtless considered an unforgivable sin, his sexual betrayal of her mother. She tells how, when she was around ten years old, her mother was incapacitated by depression, but in the autobiography, she does not reveal its cause. Richmond gossip, however, blamed the breakdown on her father's affair with a black woman of the city.[3] In Glasgow's imagination, her father became, through this cruel betrayal, the source of all cruelty, all betrayal. While in her autobiography she evidently could not bring herself to face his infidelity directly, she accuses him in other ways. He heartlessly disposed of pets that she loved as companions; he sold the farm which was her favorite retreat; he forbade her to read books that went against his principles; he "never made the slightest effort to win the affection of his children" (86). Home, for Glasgow, became a battleground between daughter and father. Yet for all that she blamed him for almost all of her "early sorrow," as she called her childhood, he was also responsible for giving her the awareness of her own being that she shaped into a weapon to use against him. In the process of finding the words to fight her father, she found her vocation.

Zora Neale Hurston's home generated a similar division of feelings. She, like Glasgow, dramatizes the tensions of her childhood through her portrayal of parents who were in all ways opposites. Home for Zora was "a big piece of ground with two big chinaberry trees shading the front gate" and the eight-room house that her father built there. Home, in a larger sense, was the town her father helped to build as well: Eatonville, Florida, an all-black town to which John Hurston journeyed as a young husband trying to make his fortune. Eatonville bore John Hurston's stamp as surely as the spacious house that he built for his family. "Later on, he was to be elected Mayor of Eatonville for three terms, and to write the local laws," Hurston boasts (15). John Hurston had been an "over-the-creek nigger" when he first met Lucy Potts; her parents disowned her when she ran away with him. Thus Zora Hurston's parents exhibited temperaments as different as Ellen Glasgow's, and like Ellen, Zora identified with the mother while she learned to hate the father.

John Hurston was a large, powerful man who could "hit ninety-seven out of a hundred with a gun" (91). More significantly for his daughter, he was a man who felt that girls were next to useless, good only "to wear out shoes and bring in nothing" (27). He expected Zora to be "meek and mild" like her older sister, but Lucy Hurston fought against training her younger daughter to be "a mealy-mouthed rag doll" when she grew up. Thus Hurston shows her mother telling the oppressive father, "Zora is my young'un, and Sarah is yours" (21). The diminutive mother had a kind of psychological power that often whittled down her husband's image of himself, for it was "a griping thing to a man—not to be able to whip his woman mentally" (92). As long as her mother lived, she offered Zora a model of determination, a will never to be "whipped" or belittled by seemingly stronger males. Yet Lucy Hurston died when Zora was nine years old: "Mama died at sundown and changed a world," she says; "that hour began my wanderings" (89). Life in her father's house became unbearable, especially when he brought home a new wife who tried to cement her place by cutting down the children. Continual struggle thus characterizes Hurston's vision of her life within her family; the battles with her father placed her emotionally on her mother's losing side; on the other hand, combatting him with his best weapon, words, gave her the means to win in the end.

While Lucy encouraged her daughter to "jump at de sun," John predicted that "somebody was going to blow me down for my sassy tongue" (21). In Eatonville, men were the ones who gathered to tell stories, who prided themselves on their "lying" skills, and who could say, as her father said, "What's de use of me taking my fist to a poor weakly thing like a woman?" (22). In *Dust Tracks,* Hurston associates the power of language, exemplified in her own "sassy tongue," with her father and with maleness generally: "he had a poetry about him that I loved. That made him a successful preacher" (91), she says in her final assessment of John Hurston. Yet she is quick to add, "But I was Mama's child." Her clearest sense of her father's role is, again, similar to Glasgow's: "Let me change a few words with him—and I am of the word-changing kind —and he was ready to change ends" (27–28). She loved and identified with her mother, but it was her father, not Lucy Hurston, who avoided Old Death, who flaunted an invincible physical presence, and whose big voice announced his proprietorship over language. Karla Holloway, in a study of Hurston's use of language, assesses the differing influences that Hurston's parents exercised on her writing: "It was as if her mother's voice dominated the psychological, and her father's image controlled the visual world of her fiction" (19). To appropriate her father's visual poetry, to exhibit it in the metaphoric language of her books, was a way to "hit ninety-nine out of a hundred with a gun," as Hurston boasted her father could do; it was, of course, to beat the patriarch at his own game.

Eudora Welty, who also provides a child's vision of home, has lived nearly all her life in her father's house, much as Ellen Glasgow did. Not unlike John Hurston in Eatonville, Christian Welty built his house in a thriving small southern town to whose prosperity he greatly contributed. In *One Writer's Beginnings,* Welty remembers two childhood homes, both dominated by her father. She opens her autobiography by saying, "In our house on North Congress Street in Jackson, Mississippi, where I was born, the oldest of three children, in 1909, we grew up to the striking of clocks" (3). And clocks, we soon learn, are symbolic of Mr. Welty, who "loved all instruments that would instruct and fascinate." On the family's return from any trip, he would always go "from room to room re-starting all the clocks" (68). The second house, her residence from 1925 to the present time, was one that he had built in the same year that he oversaw the construction of his insurance building, the "new Lamar Life home office building on Capitol Street" with its clock tower that could be read "from all over town" (82–83). Welty describes her second childhood home in these terms: "The house was on a slight hill (my mother never could see the hill) covered with its original forest pines, on a gravel road then a little out from town, and was built in a style very much of its day, of stucco and brick and beams in the Tudor style. We had moved in, and Mother was laying out the garden" (83). Even in this seemingly straightforward vignette the images reflect oppositional pulls that Welty's parents came to represent: her father was the keeper of time, her mother the gardener; he was the life insurance man who distrusted risks while she was the mountain-born, daring one who would naturally be disdainful of anything that Jackson, Mississippi, called "a hill." Consistently Welty suggests that her childhood was divided between two very different parental philosophies: "he the optimist was the one who was prepared for the worst, and she the pessimist was the dare-devil" (45), their daughter comments wryly.

Welty takes a gentler approach to her parents than the two earlier southern women writers. Ellen Glasgow and Zora Neale Hurston made their fathers villains, to a certain extent because they were the controllers, the survivors, the big voices in their worlds. Mothers exercised strong emotional influences yet did not have the power or will to guide their daughters into the future. Welty's parents, on the other hand, complemented rather than opposed each other with their "different gifts," as Welty saw them, yet her father's influence dominated, at least in her backward-glancing version of her childhood. He was the one who kept the time, who "had the accurate knowledge of the weather," whose "sense of direction was unassailable." Each of the three sections of her autobiography begins with an image of her father. The striking of clocks in "Listening" is the autobiography's first sound. Welty goes on to say that it was her father's influence that made his children "time-minded all our lives" (3). In "Learning to See," the narrative begins with a summer trip by "touring car," a trip in which "mother was the navigator" (43). Still her father controlled the journey, for Welty says, "Riding behind my father I could see that the road had him by the shoulders. . . . I inherited his nervous energy in the way I can't stop writing on a story" (44). The third section, "Finding a Voice," begins with a train trip that Eudora took with her father when she was a young girl. The two were kindred souls in their love of journeying, although her father's way of knowing would ultimately be rejected by his daughter: "My father knew our way mile by mile; by day or by night, he knew where we were" (73), Welty says. In the omniscience that Welty grants him, her father was the namer, the builder, the one who "put it all into the frame of regularity, predictability" as a "fatherly gift" (74). The mother that we meet in *One Writer's Beginnings* remains somehow elusive, unavailable, even unyielding. Her father perhaps regulated the world too efficiently, without allowing for the sense of mystery that the daughter had to learn to trust, but the mother took away by giving too much. "All my life," Welty says in one particularly stark statement, "I continued to feel that bliss for me would have to imply my mother's deprivation or sacrifice" (19). Welty, then, like Glasgow and Hurston, associates the mother with suffering and sacrifice. The father, more vitally present and always in charge, offers a model of forbidden or inaccessible power that constitutes a challenge. No wonder, then, that all three writers, as daughters, were torn between longing for the father's self-sufficiency and guilt for the mother's self-denial.

Glasgow, Hurston, and Welty begin their autobiographical journeys by confronting home, parents, and community. In each case, tension between father and mother defines the child, who turns between two kinds of knowledge, two sets of influences, two choices of self-image. Glasgow denied the father, who for her represented the stifling of both sympathy and creativity. In *The Woman Within,* she relates that when she pestered her father with "the monosyllable Why? Why? Why?," he "would pay me a new penny to stop asking questions" (25). Francis Glasgow objected, when Ellen was older, to her reading Gibbon and Darwin, yet his "righteous rage" simply stimulated her to follow any direction that she felt he disliked: "Father had estranged me, without thinking a child could be estranged," she explains, so that "now all the tumult of unreason provoked only a clash of two wills equally strong." Her credo became, "my mind is my own!" (92–93). Ironically, of course, even Glasgow's protest took its shape from her father's control. In her own iron-willed pursuit of the kinds of knowledge he wanted to deny her, she reflected his molding and nature much more than her mother's.

Hurston, like Glasgow, longed to see herself as "Mama's child," yet she was a "word changer" (given to talking back) and a traveler in her father's image, as she admits at least once. Responding to her mother's fear of her wandering ways, she comments, "I don't know why it never occurred to her to connect my tendency with my father, who didn't have a thing on his mind but this town and the next one. . . . Some children are just bound to take after their fathers in spite of women's prayers" (32). Taking after her father, both in his wanderlust and in his gift with words, was a direction that Hurston must have followed with ambivalent feelings. In her last references to John Hurston, she pictures him as a man defeated, "dragging around like a stepped-on worm" (126). In emasculating her father with this example of "specifying," Hurston perhaps acknowledged her deepest debt to the man who was himself a master preacher. The "word-changing" daughter here changes places with the most powerful word-wielder in her community.[4]

Welty, unlike Glasgow or Hurston, did not bring direct anger to bear upon the recollection of her early relationships, even though she writes of her family that "our tempers were all strong and intense" (38). She seems to have needed to internalize the tensions that rippled under the quiet surfaces of the childhood life she describes: "my anger was at myself, every time," she confesses. She goes so far as to say that "as a fiction writer, I am minus an adversary—except, of course, that of time" (38). Yet in these words she evokes the one image, time, that she most closely associated with her father, whose obsession with regularity, with demystifying the world, obviously troubled her.[5] With her mother, she is less circumspect, as she discusses how she was made to feel guilty for wanting some escape from her family's overprotectiveness. In one of her most revealing statements about her parents' influence, Welty says, "It took me a long time to manage the independence, for I loved those who protected me—and I wanted inevitably to protect them back. I have never managed to handle the guilt" (19–20). "Fierce independence," she adds, "was my chief inheritance from my mother" (60). Yet in recognizing this inheritance, Welty also uncovers a reason for her ambivalence toward her mother. For although Mrs. Welty possessed an "independent spirit," she tried to keep Eudora from exercising her own freedom: "It was what she so agonizingly tried to protect me from. . . . It was what we shared, it made the strongest bond between us and the strongest tension" (60). Welty, then, like Glasgow and Hurston, discovered and embodied in her parents oppositions that constituted an artistic challenge. The tensions that for all three writers defined life at home led to inward journeys. And in these journeys, the daughter transformed all of the relationships of the past by creating a separate, unique voice.

Leaving Home: The Inward Journey

Finding language and using it to create stories constituted each of these writers' essential journey away from home. In *The Woman Within, Dust Tracks,* and *One Writer's Beginnings,* the child's discovery of a writer's voice gave her a secret power over a world otherwise filled with threatening silences. Glasgow calls the fourth chapter of her autobiography, "I Become a Writer." From this terse announcement, we might expect an account of how Glasgow published her first novel, but instead we learn how, as the first sentence proclaims, "In my seventh summer I became a writer" (36). Here the young Ellen is shown trying her hand at making "po'try." Glasgow, I think, has a deeper intention than simply displaying how a precocious child found her lifelong purpose in verse-making. More important is how writing dramatically changed her relationship with her family. When her sisters found her poems and laughingly read them aloud, their theft of her voice drove her to hide her new identity. While her sisters meant no harm in giggling over her verses, she felt estranged. In this way her vocation took her at an early age past the boundaries of home. Significantly, the poem that Glasgow places into the text of her autobiography as Child Ellen's first verse contains images of wandering, voices belonging to angels, and a father who sits above in the role of authenticator:

> Drift from this land of mist and snow,
> Drift to the land where I long to go,
> Leaving behind me the world's sad choices,
> Hearing alone the angels' voices,
> At the foot of my Father's throne.
>
> (37)

Glasgow does not comment on the way that her simple verse foretells future struggles, yet she offers it as evidence of her childhood self as a hero, excluded, isolated, roaming in search of a new home.

Hearing her verses read aloud drove Glasgow to an outward silence, but also to an absolute interior riot of voicing/writing: "I wrote always in secret, but I wrote ceaselessly in dim corners, under beds, or, in the blessed summer days, under the deep shrubbery and beneath low-hanging boughs" (41). Here, as we have seen before, Glasgow projects her transformation through settings that, in their progression, take the writer out of hiding and into nature itself. The adult writer, firmly in control of her memories, performs openly as the child was afraid to do. The only person in the child's world who "suspected but did not speak" of this "dark stream of identity," the vocation of writer that young Ellen had seized, was, not surprisingly, her mother (41).

In writing about her early forays into the forbidden world of words, Glasgow associates her vocation with silence and also with wandering away from home. Before she began to write, the habit of story-telling already formed a central part of Glasgow's life, she tells us. As a preschool-age child, she wandered the fields of her farm or the streets of Richmond with her beloved black "Mammy." Always these "wandering adventures" were associated with stories: "we sought adventures, not only in the tales we spun at night," she says, "but even in the daytime, when we roamed, hand-in-hand, in search of the fresh and the strange" (18). The "actual adventures" of her jaunts with Mammy were not as thrilling as the story of a hero, "Little Willie," whom Ellen and her nurse created. Glasgow chose a young male as an imaginary friend, and with him she was chased by bears, joined a circus, discovered buried treasure—in other words, with him she played out in imagination, accompanied by an equally imaginative, yet illiterate, black woman servant, dreams denied to women, to Blacks, to the powerless and inarticulate of her society.

In *Dust Tracks on a Road,* young Zora Hurston forged paths away from home similar to those that the child Ellen Glasgow traced. Like Glasgow, she felt set apart from others: "They were not like me and mine" (34). She enraged her father by asking not for a doll at Christmas, but for a riding horse which would carry her to the end of the world. She sat on top of the gatepost in front of her house and asked passersby (usually "white travelers," she says) to let her "go a piece of the way" with them (45). She wanted to play with boys instead of girls, because boys "got into fights"; when this pleasure was denied, she was "driven inward" (40). Hurston tells us that she cannot remember when she began to make up stories, but that from an early age, she imitated the "lying" that she heard the men practicing at the store. The consequence was punishment. Her grandmother reacted to her made-up tales by insisting that her mother "break her . . . Grab her! Wring her coat tails over her head and wear out a handful of peach hickories on her back-side!" (71–72). Hurston, faced with this kind of conspiracy to silence her, responded in the same way that Glasgow did: "I could keep my inventions to myself, which is what I did most of the time" (72–73). Their families' attempts to turn these daughters away from their natural instincts for self-expression succeeded only in turning them inward, where they found ways to develop voices and visions.

While Glasgow created her imaginary playmate, Little Willie, to carry her to freedom, Hurston made Miss Corn-Shuck and Mr. Sweet-Smell —in reality, as Hurston explains, an inside "chunk" of corn left from her mother's shucking pile and a cake of sweet soap from her mother's drawer. Miss Corn-Shuck came first for her creator, in an interesting gender twist of the Adam and Eve myth. Transferring her own sense of isolation onto her created playmate, Hurston made Mr. Sweet-Smell, she says, only after "Miss Corn-Shuck got lonesome for some company" (73). Her imaginary creations "stayed around the house for years," Hurston says, "holding funerals and almost weddings and taking trips with me to where the sky met the ground" (77). Thus Hurston, looking back on her dawning sense of vocation, associates storytelling with wandering, inwardness, secrecy, silence, and community rituals. Her creativity sets her apart from that community while it also allows her to see herself as goddess: "My soul was with the gods and my body in the village" (56), she says.

Welty, like Hurston, shaped her material to give it a heroic cast. She defines "Finding a Voice" as the culmination of her quest as a writer, making up the last, triumphant portion of her story. Yet the process of achieving a voice and becoming a writer began with "listening" and "learning to see." Listening to the sounds of her home, especially her parents' voices, and learning to see their full lives stretching out over time brought her an artist's knowledge of what makes a story. Her parents' lives led her to her vocation in intricate, unpredictable ways. For example, her father's attention to time "was good at least for a future fiction writer, being able to learn so penetratingly, and almost first of all, about chronology" (3). His fascination with weather developed in her "a strong meteorological sensibility," so that "in years ahead when I wrote stories, atmosphere took its influential role from the start" (4). Her mother's reading gave her a love of books, although she reports that the voice she heard when her mother read "isn't my mother's voice" (11). A story or poem, she learned, had its own voice, "human, but inward, and it is inwardly that I listen to it" (11). Listening, then, could take the child Eudora away from the parent's voice and into an inner world of her own determining.

In learning to see and listening, Welty's childhood was a process of differentiation, less violent yet no less essential than the process that separated Glasgow and Hurston from their parents. Isolation, Welty found, could come even in the midst of great intimacy, teaching a crucial lesson. Welty tells how, at a time when she was confined home during a childhood illness, her parents kept her in their bedroom during the evenings. They let her fall asleep in their bed while, on the other side of the room, they talked over the news of the day. "What was thus dramatically made a present to me," Welty says, "was the secure sense of the hidden observer" (20). She was "present in the room with the chief secret"— her parents' own shared, private lives, available to her through conflicting feelings of exclusion and participation. The separation, secretness, and distancing that Welty experienced on this occasion developed into her chosen method as a writer. She tells us that "a conscious act grew out of this by the time I began to write stories: getting my distance, a prerequisite of my understanding of human events, is the way I begin work" (20–21). Her parents' habits and talk could show her aspects of her art, but only distance could generate the understanding that allowed the practice of it.

Getting her distance was not always easy, however. Welty reveals something of the strain that her family's protecting love imposed when she writes of what journeys meant within that closed circle: "Taking trips tore all of us up inside, for they seemed, each journey away from home, something that might have been less selfishly undertaken. . . . The torment and guilt—the torment of having the loved one go, the guilt of being the loved one gone—comes into my fiction as it did and does into my life" (94). Yet Welty did not veer from the course away from home, no matter how painful. She saw in travelling a metaphor for her writing: "trips were wholes unto themselves. They were stories" (68), she announces. Trips heralded "direction, movement, development, change," which were essential to stories and to her own growth as a writer. Taking on the guilt of "the loved one gone" was the risk and the price, willingly paid.

Storytelling became, then, for these three southern women writers, a form of essential journeying away from home. What they learned, as part of their discovery of a writer's vocation, was that the essential journeys of life were inward ones that led to self-possession, the prerequisite for self-expression. Wandering and trips made "tracks" that were outward signs of inward motion. Glasgow, Hurston, and Welty all affirmed the value to their art of travels into unknown inner realms of mind. Glasgow tells us that what she learned from all her reading of others was that "Truth to art became in the end simple fidelity to one's own inner vision" (125). Often separation marked the onset of such vision. The death of Glasgow's mother turned her away from externals. She writes, "It is more than forty years now since she died, yet a part of me seems still to live on, in that hour, in that moment. A part of me, buried but alive, was held there. . . . Yet some other self stands in the center of that desolate room, looks through the blurred window-panes, and still watches, without knowing what it watches, two sparrows quarreling in the slow rain on a roof" (83–84). Two selves—one buried in the past, one now watching and making poetry out of what it sees—are equally alive, as Glasgow envisions them, mingling inner and outer worlds and past and present images of identity.

Hurston, like Glasgow, experienced in her mother's death an alienation that drove her to inner vision. Emerging from this crisis, she became forever a wanderer, "not so much in geography, but in time. Then not so much in time as in spirit" (89). Thus Hurston's autobiography, like Glasgow's, charts a journey away from home that is basically a journey into herself. Chapter 4 of *Dust Tracks,* entitled "Inside Search," outlines this journey in a pattern of dreams that she had when she was "not more than seven years old" (56). The dreams were actually mental pictures, landscapes shaped by a mind assimilating losses and disconnections from others. The child Zora saw herself as an orphan, she stood "beside a dark pool of water" watching "a huge fish move slowly away," she crossed many tracks to board a train, she went to "a shotgun-built house that needed a new coat of white paint" (57–58). While Hurston speaks out as the autobiographical narrator to say that "Time was to prove the truth of my visions," within the narrative itself she makes no sustained attempt to tie the twelve images to actual events in her life. The title of the chapter indicates to us that these "prophecies" were symbols belonging to an imaginative, interior world and not a rational, chronological one. Hurston says that she told no one of her visions, for "they would laugh me off as a story-teller" (58), which was, of course, what her "inside search" was making her. From the moment that Hurston discovered this extra dimension of her existence, she "stood apart within," as she puts it. The child who dreamed and gathered images into a defining pattern for her life was on her way to becoming the woman writer whose most important searches would always be interior ones.

In *One Writer's Beginnings,* journeys are a basic metaphor for inward struggles to find a voice. In "Listening," we learn very early of the electric train that Mr. Welty set up "as soon as the boys [Welty's brothers] attained anywhere near the right age" (5). Here, the daughter was excluded from the adventures connected to this wonderful toy, "running around and around its figure eight." The girl child will have to create her own train, her own track, her own interior patterns of adventure. "Learning to See" is organized around the family's summer trip to West Virginia and Ohio, where Welty watched her parents looking back to their pasts and meeting up with the early dreams and sorrows that had shaped the future. Here again, she could only watch, not participate in, another's journey, yet internalized watching showed her a path that she could take in stories to come. In "Finding a Voice," Welty begins to follow that path. The section starts with the train trip that she took, as a child, with her father: the two "were in no other respect so congenial" as in the way that they both "hungered" for the knowledge of unknown worlds that their journey afforded. Later in the section, Welty, now a grown woman, boards a train leaving Jackson, in a simple but dramatic act which announces that she has, indeed, found her voice as she has found the will to leave home: "I had left to arrive at some future and secret joy, at what was unknown, and what was now in New York, waiting to be discovered. My joy was connected with writing" (94). New York, an outer destination, signifies an inner goal, the mastery of a writer's voice. Thus Welty's most important journeys, like Glasgow's and Hurston's, were all interior. Even in her girlhood train trip with her father, she had realized that, although she was looking out on a real world from the train window, what she took in was something of her own making. Telling of people out in fields picking blackberries, she remarks, "I never saw with the thought of their continuing to be there just the same after we were out of sight. For now, and for a long while to come, I was proceeding in fantasy" (75). And one of this train-rider's final perceptions is that "It is our inward journey that leads us through time—forward or back, seldom in a straight line, most often spiraling" (102). Like Glasgow and Hurston, Welty looked inward more than away to find her voice, for, as her last sentence reads, "all serious daring starts from within" (104).

Returning Home: The Connecting Voice

The final question becomes, for these prodigal-daughter writers, how to connect the journey away with the journey back, how to join interior searching for identity with the quest for worlds beyond self that must also be navigated and assimilated into a coherent vision. In *Women's Ways of Knowing*, the authors (Belenky, Clinchy, Goldberger, and Tarule) interviewed more than one hundred women in order to chart how their subjects came to know themselves and the world. They grouped "women's perspectives on knowing" into five "epistemological categories" ranging from "silence" to "constructed knowledge." The third "way of knowing," labeled "subjectivist," constitutes a course of seeking based on "woman's discovery of personal authority and truth" (76). In their section on subjectivist knowing, the description of how women begin to seek an inner self applies to the process that Glasgow, Hurston, and Welty trace in their autobiographies. "In many ways," the authors state, "these women are like the youths in fairy tales (as we recall, usually male), who set out from the family homestead to make their way in the world, discovering themselves in the process" (77). Women at this position "experience a wrenching away of the familiar contexts and relationships within which the old identity has been embedded" (81). As they turn "inward to listen to the 'still small voice,'" they find "a new and fascinating object for study: the self" (84–85). This turning inward is what we have witnessed in our southern women writers' descriptions of buried selves, disconnected dreams, and distancing journeys.

What the authors of *Women's Ways of Knowing* stress about the "subjectivist" period is that "the predominant learning mode" at this stage applies "inward listening and watching," acts which represent a "primary means . . . for articulation and differentiation of the self" (85). The chief risk of this perspective is that a "strictly subjectivist epistemology" can contribute to isolation, loneliness, even despair among those women who have "not found bridges back to other people" (84). Like the women interviewed in this work, Glasgow, Hurston, and Welty listened carefully to parents' voices, yet learned to recognize signs of worlds beyond the fixed, circling roads of home; they also learned to look inward to articulate their own stories and differentiate themselves from family "others." Finally, from their inside positions, all three women used writing to build bridges back to people and places, known and unknown, that made up broad artistic territories.

The last category in *Women's Ways of Knowing* is "constructed knowing," a strategy that enables women to build bridges connecting themselves to others and to outer worlds. In this position, women begin "to integrate knowledge that they felt intuitively was personally important with knowledge they had learned from others"; they begin "weaving together the strands of rational and emotive thought" and "integrating objective and subjective knowing" (134). We watch Ellen Glasgow's arrival at this position in *The Woman Within* when she is able to say, "I had planned, in these memoirs, to deal only with my intellectual changes and pursuits, with the continuous search for a creed. . . . In looking back, I see, now, that my emotional and my intellectual lives formed a single strand, and could not be divided. So closely were they intertwined that I could not tell where one began in pure feeling, and the other ended in pure speculation" (56). Our last concern with the autobiographies of Glasgow, Hurston, and Welty involves watching how the vocation of writer took them back to the most important "others" in their lives—their families—through acts of connection, integration, or, in other words, homecoming.

Glasgow left her father's house, travelled widely, educated herself in spite of little formal schooling, and began a writing career that seemed to separate her quite decisively from the traditions of southern culture that her father and Richmond represented. In an early statement concerning southern literature, Glasgow bewailed its lack of "blood and irony" (*CM* 28). In *The Woman Within* she tells us that she went to New York to find a publisher because "Southerners did not publish, did not write, did not read" (105). Yet in New York she was disappointed when she met some of the leading "literary" (her quotation marks) men of the 1890s; "I did not like to be patronized," she said, "and I had not come so far from home in search of benevolent old gentlemen. That was a product in which the South was never found wanting." She adds pointedly, "And more than anything else, I wanted the right to be heard" (110). Glasgow distanced herself from a South that she first defined as a stifling fatherland, clearly associating her identity as a writer with an escape from a patriarchal home that would not listen to her voice. Experiencing problems with progressive deafness during these years, she went so far as to say that she herself could hear better in New York than she could in Richmond (137). Further, she at first rejected the South as an imaginative home for her stories; her first two novels (*The Descendant,* 1897, and *Phases of an Inferior Planet,* 1898) are set primarily in New York City. Glasgow realized, however, that these two works were "experimental failures," admitting "we write better . . . when we write of places we know, and of a background with which we are familiar. A guidebook is a poor scene for a novel" (*WW* 129–30).

Beginning with her third novel (*The Voice of the People,* 1900) Ellen Glasgow, at least in her fiction, returned and stayed home. The novel was the first in what she describes, in *The Woman Within,* as a "series of books which would deal with the Virginian background," a "design" which she worked out in the next twenty years (129). The authorial posture that she strikes in explaining this series is that of a novelist largely "at home" both literally and in terms of the themes and settings of her fiction. Anne Goodwyn Jones measures the result when she writes, "That Ellen Glasgow was a southerner not only by birth and rearing, but by some fairly deep level of choice, is clear not just from her geographical roamings and homings. It is also clear in the springs of her art. Unlike the novelist who must leave to gain detachment, Glasgow had to come home" (228). One statement from *The Woman Within* shows dramatically that Glasgow ultimately understood how deeply her identity and purposes as a writer were connected to her home: "if I could criticize," she says, thinking about the South's innocence and sentimentality, "it was not because I had escaped from the elegiac tone that surrounded me" (104). Confrontation and connection were better positions from which to criticize than was escape, as her next words show: "in the South there was not only adolescence to outgrow, there was an insidious sentimental tradition to live down. I had been brought up in the midst of it; I was a part of it, or it was a part of me" (104). Glasgow here integrates self and home, reordering the relationships of the past in a way that provides both power and vital connection.

Ellen Glasgow went back to Richmond to claim her artistic inheritance; Zora Neale Hurston returned to Eatonville for the same purpose, after a more complete break with her family and her own past self. In the years following her mother's death, Hurston felt completely disconnected. Sent to live with various relatives and friends because of her father's new wife, Hurston felt that she was, during this period, "forever shifting," and it was a "wordless feeling" (*Dust Tracks* 116–17). She writes, "I had always thought I would be in some lone, arctic wasteland with no one under the sound of my voice. I found the cold, the desolate solitude, and earless silences, but I discovered that all geography was within me" (115). As Susan Willis says, "[Hurston's] fear as a teller of tales is the 'earless silence.' The image captures the dread felt by an untried black woman, who would be a writer, of casting her words into a void" (38). The bridge between "earless silence" and an audience, people who would hear her voice, came with a kind of internal discovery of the geography of home. Her wanderings away took her to Barnard College where she studied anthropology with Dr. Franz Boas, whom she called

"Papa Franz" (170). "It was a long step for the waif of Eatonville" (172), she comments in *Dust Tracks*. It was ultimately a homeward step as well, for Boas arranged a fellowship that allowed her to "go south and collect Negro folklore" (171). As she drove towards the Deep South, she visited with family members along the way and learned about her father's last days (her autobiography had not mentioned his death, or indeed even his name, since she had shown herself leaving his house after a violent fight with her stepmother). Thus she returned to the South fatherless, yet on a mission to claim her inheritance, the stories, songs, and superstitions that her father had passed around, with the other menfolk, on the store porch.

Mules and Men, the folklore collection published in 1935 as the first fruits of Hurston's homecoming, has been called "the most engaging, genuine, and skillfully written book in the field of folklore" (*MM* xxiii). Robert Hemenway measures its importance in these terms: "The tales here are *not* the quaint, childish entertainments of a primitive tribe. They are the complex cultural communications permitted an oppressed people, their school lessons, their heroic biographies, their psychic savings banks, their children's legacies" (*MM* xxii). The form and voice that Hurston created for *Mules and Men* gives her a share in that legacy. *Mules and Men* is framed as an autobiography; Hurston, the collector of the tales, is a character in this story of the transmission of a culture. In part 1, "Folk Tales," she drives into Eatonville and salutes the old power group sitting on the store porch. "Hello, boys," she says (9). Yet a transformation takes place when the storytelling begins: Zora moves the party to the front porch of her friend Armetta's house, where the tellers, men and women both, eat gingerbread and drink buttermilk in a kind of communion, a ceremony connecting men and women, past and present, in storytelling ritual. By her return, and through "constructed knowing," the woman folklorist establishes her voice and connects it to the voices of other black men and women, named and name-giving, sharers in equal portion in the core experiences that tell a people who they are.

In *Mules and Men,* Hurston both receives and transmits "the word," embedded first in the scenes, places, and people she had known when she was, as she names herself in the book's introduction, "Lucy Hurston's daughter, Zora" (3). Explaining why she decided to begin collecting tales at home in Florida, she says, "I realized that I was new myself, so it looked sensible for me to choose familiar ground" (3). Thus in one sense she returned home an initiate, ready to find her past on a different footing, through a different, connected way of knowing. Toward the end of the collection, Hurston fashions her own unique theory of the biblical father, Moses, as she introduces the idea of "hoodoo" that formed an important thread of black religion. Moses, she says, "made a nation and a book"; his power, for her, resided in his knowledge of God's "making words." To be a word maker, a book maker, is to have divine power, she suggests, the kind of power, of course, that she was in the process of illustrating on the page of the book her reader held. She adds that "Moses never would have stood before the Burning Bush, if he had not married Jethro's daughter" (194). Through this observation, daughterhood becomes empowered for Lucy and John Hurston's child. Women— daughters, mothers, and storytellers—preside over powerful worlds of their own making in the culminating mythology which *Mules and Men* presents. Thus in one sense, although Hurston was an "initiate," owner of a new self as she returned home, she was also presider and presenter, a priestess affirming her people's and her own connections to their communities and culture.

One Writer's Beginnings, in its overall organization, comes remarkably close to duplicating the movement from silent listening to integrated knowing that *Women's Ways of Knowing* charts. The concept of the "subjectivist position" is a dual one through which women both "watch and listen to themselves and begin to notice inner contradictions" and also "watch and listen to others and begin to draw comparisons between their own and other people's experience" (85). Welty's perspective in "Listening" and "Learning to See" clearly engages her in this mode of knowing. In "Finding a Voice," Welty moves from her role of watching, listening child to her role as speaker, becoming the author who, she says, "remains and needs to remain at his private remove" (87). Using this perspective, Welty shows herself to be a "constructivist" knower who wants "to embrace all the pieces of the self in some ultimate sense of the whole—daughter, friend, mother, lover, nurturer, thinker, artist, advocate" (*Women's Ways* 137). Writing, which for Welty also means voicing, is a connecting strategy: "writing a story or a novel is one way of discovering *sequence* in experience," she says, so that "connections slowly emerge" (90). In this way, for Welty, all the pieces of the self come together.

In *Women's Ways of Knowing,* constructivists are defined not only as connected knowers but, more significantly, as "passionate" knowers who "enter into a union with that which is to be known" (141). Passion, along with memory, is the word that Welty uses in "Finding a Voice" to indicate her way of knowing the world, which was also her way of travelling home. She writes that she did not find "the world out there revealing" until she began to write in her twenties, at a time when "*memory* had become attached to seeing, love had added itself to discovery, and because I recognized in my own continuing longing to keep going, the need I carried inside myself to know—the apprehension, first, and then the passion, to connect myself to it" (76). The whole of *One Writer's Beginnings,* perhaps even the whole of Welty's fiction, represents her passion to connect herself to the world through voice and memory. That passion, she realized, took her home, to the parents and the childhood from which she had achieved her necessary distance. To the "inward journey that leads us through time" she gave the name "confluence," for her a "wonderful word" naming what memory made possible. Heading home, Welty found that the confluence which "makes up the human memory" is capable of giving moments when "all that is remembered joins, and lives—the old and the young, the past and the present, the living and the dead" (104). Confluence, joining, attachment, connection are her names for her inward journey.

In their autobiographies and, as we shall see, in their fiction, Glasgow, Hurston, and Welty created themselves by turning inward and then reaching outward. As daughters, they were shaped by often conflicting parental influences. As travellers, they found themselves most fully in inward journeys. As authors, they discovered themselves in remembering home, and in remembering themselves, discovered home. Always, they were transformed by the knowledge that they gained. These prodigal daughters, in finding their voices, claimed their heritage, and home, far from being a safe harbor at the end of the journey, became itself the daring writer's beginning.

CHAPTER THREE

The Voice in the Garden

Creating Women
in the Modern Southern Novel

In letters that Harriet Jacobs, a former slave, and Catherine Hammond, a widowed plantation mistress, wrote after the end of the Civil War, one striking image asserts itself, the image of woman creating. It is an image that archetypically connects these two women, and indeed all women, to the figure of the mother goddess who, Joseph Campbell tells us, was seen by the earliest societies as "the first planter" (101), "the personification of the energy that gives birth to forms and nourishes forms" (167). Catherine Hammond, who became the head of her household when James Henry Hammond died in 1864, wrote to her brother-in-law, Marcus Hammond, in September of 1865, apprising him of a world transformed not just by the war and its aftermath but by her own new position. While she mentions that it was hard to "restrain a burst of complaint at my change of circumstances," she sees, for the most part, "only cause for thankfulness." As she lists her blessings, she includes the fact that "the crop promises well," and a few lines later she reiterates, "meat and corn both low, but the new crop coming in" (144). Close to two years later, in April of 1867, Harriet Jacobs found her way back to Edenton, North Carolina, and the home she had fled, as a slave, twenty-five years earlier. Shortly after this homecoming, she wrote to a northern friend as she sat in the house that her grandmother had left to her. In her letter, she speaks of her somber memories of the seven years

that she hid in her grandmother's house while she sought a way to free
not only herself but also her son and daughter. Yet in her letter she looks
to the future more than at the past, as she writes, "I have spent much
of my time on the Plantations distributing seed and trying to teach the
women to make Yankee gardens. they (sic) plant everything to mature
in the summer, like their corn and cotton fields" (250).

   In both letters, despair is replaced with hope, cycles of renewal are
confidently forecast, rhythms of sowing and reaping, of seed-time and
harvest-time, are celebrated—and by women, women who had been
slaves to men and to a system rigidly controlled by men. The letters recall the figures of Demeter and Persephone, mother and daughter, who
in early agricultural societies were often considered two aspects of one
powerful goddess of fertility and renewal. In the Greco-Roman myth,
we recall, Demeter is the great "Grain Mother," the directress and protectress of "the plowing, the sowing, the threshing and reaping, and the
storage of the harvest" (Sjoo and Mor, *Cosmic Mother* 166). Her daughter
Persephone is, in one respect, the grain harvest itself; she disappears
seasonally, spending long wintry months in the underworld, where she
presides over the realm of Death. In the spring, returned to her mother,
she becomes again the maiden, and the two reunited bring new life to the
Earth. Demeter, who searches for her daughter in the male-dominated
world of death, is in one sense searching for and mourning a lost part of
herself. During this time of separation from self, no crops can grow; the
world sinks into barrenness and despair which end only when mother
and daughter, the two split forms of feminine identity, rejoin and in their
union return the earth to spring. The process is cyclical as well as re-
generative, involving recurring patterns of birth, separation, search, and
new growth. When we think of Demeter and Persephone as two aspects
of a unitary, self-sufficient, and self-regenerative female being, mother
and maiden in one identity, then we better understand woman as creative force, containing within herself the processes of life and death. In
order to create, she must lose herself, yet she must then search heroically
to find and be reunited with the part of her that has been sacrificed and
imprisoned. The ideal woman goddess figure, then, endures the hell of
death, separation, incompleteness, in order to bring herself to fruition.
Yet her discovery of herself is not only a personal victory, but a commu-

nal one; in finding herself, she transfigures and rejuvenates the world, making possible a return to an original garden of wholeness and love. The writings of Catherine Hammond and Harriet Jacobs, seedbearers and planters as they became, dramatize this ritual story.

Monica Sjoo and Barbara Mor tell us in *The Great Cosmic Mother* (1987) that "feminists have read the Demeter-Persephone myth as a paradigm of contemporary woman, struggling to escape the death clutch of patriarchy in a search for her original, fruitful self. As the grieving, determined mother she descends to the Underworld—into social rebellion, role-reversals, personal madness, the dark journeys of introspection and disintegration that precede creative, visionary power—to rediscover her own soul, retrieve the joyous daughter of self-determining life" (167). The stories that Harriet Jacobs and Catherine Hammond told in part 1 chart Demeter-Persephone's dual journey of descent and discovery. Their South was founded upon a patriarchal system that made all women daughters, defined as perpetual dependents, servants of the progenitor-creator, the father, the husband, or the master—the man in any case who demanded or dispensed the fruits of women's bodies and women's labor by virtue of his maleness. Hammond and Jacobs found creative freedom only after they escaped from two different yet related prisons wherein they were defined almost exclusively by their sexuality. The myth of Demeter and Persephone suggests the ideal of mother and daughter merged in one being whose creative power resides in the generational force suggested by that merger; it is a power that is lost to the mother-daughter-woman when she exists only or primarily to fulfill men's sexual needs. As Hammond and Jacobs changed from silence to speech, from women defined sexually by men to women naming themselves and cultivating their own gardens, they initiated the quest that we have been tracing for new definitions of the figure of southern daughter.

Women novelists of the last several generations have shaped stories about women characters who begin their quests from the position of patriarchally defined daughter, yet who proceed to discover creative power beyond traditional roles. Breaking away from parental or communal expectations creates a rupture for these women characters, not only between themselves and their families, but within themselves. Descent into self-doubt, experiences of separation from family and from self, lead to discoveries that enable these women to identify within themselves the source of their creativity. In the pages that follow we celebrate several of these stories of women's search for wholeness. We will hear the voice of Persephone, the daughter trapped in darkness, but also the voice of Demeter, mourning and searching for her lost daughter; in each writer we will hear the voice of the two goddesses combined, as the woman author announces, through the act of creating a whole woman character, the successful end of a quest in reunion. The title "creating women" has two references: first, to three southern novelists engaged in the act of creating through the writing voice, and second, to characters in their novels who face the challenge of creating voices within families or communities that expect them to fulfill the role of silent daughter. The novelists are women who, in their time and place, have broken new literary ground: Ellen Glasgow, Zora Neale Hurston, and Eudora Welty. The characters who, for me, best represent their concern for women's gifts of creation are Glasgow's Dorinda Oakley of *Barren Ground* (1925), Hurston's Janie Crawford of *Their Eyes Were Watching God* (1937), and Welty's Laurel McKelva of *The Optimist's Daughter* (1972).[1] Each novel illuminates its author's personal struggles with voice. The woman character initiates Demeter's quest to find and integrate self; this quest indicates the direction not only of the character's fictional story but of the author's autobiographical story as well.[2]

All three novels are patterned in cyclic sequences that move chronologically but also in recurring, spiraling directions. Gestures, such as gazing at horizons or reaching for a flower; patterns of actions, such as falling asleep and waking refreshed or moving from a dark room out into open air; social occasions, particularly weddings and funerals; natural events, such as storms, sunrises, seasonal changes—all of these both reflect and give rise to new perceptions because they are repeated in renewing, cumulative designs. Each work has its own way of extending time over the period of one whole life or even several generations. *Barren Ground* follows Dorinda Oakley over a thirty-year period, from age twenty to fifty, yet the presentation of her life is not so much linear as seasonal; at every stage she goes through alternating periods of energy and listlessness. Writing of the novel's "sense of time" in the preface included in her essay collection, *A Certain Measure,* Glasgow said, "Leaves budding, leaves falling, sun or snow, rain or dust, youth or age, life or death—this eternal sequence must place the tone of the narrative, and sustain the gradually lengthening effect of duration. Not the landscape alone, but the living human figures must reflect the slow rhythm and pause of the seasons" (159). *Their Eyes Were Watching God* develops a similar rhythmic sense of Janie's life, timed by her relationships with three men. Hurston begins with Janie's return, as a widow in her forties, to her home in Eatonville, Florida. There, she tells her life's story to an old friend, returning in her narrative to the moment of her sexual awakening, then reconstructing years that took her through three marriages and finally to the independence that makes the telling of her story possible. *The Optimist's Daughter* shows Laurel McKelva Hand, like Janie a widow in her forties, returning to her father during his last illness. Three of the novel's four sections deal with his funeral and the three days that follow, so the actual time frame of the story is short. Yet Welty's concern is to force Laurel into a confrontation with time through memory, so in memory her character must travel back not only through her own life but also through her parents' lives together. All three women characters are thus quite literally daughters of time, carrying the weight of the past into new confrontations with home and family.

In their novels Glasgow, Hurston, and Welty are concerned ultimately with questions of control and power as the tools of creation. Their inventive manipulations of time—what Glasgow called "the most important problem that confronts the writer of fiction" (*CM* 159)—are designed in part to demonstrate their mastery as authors. In other organizational aspects, too, we see the novelist's strokes, not obtrusively, yet still conspicuously—the storyteller's hand, her role as builder and framer, is everywhere present in the structure itself. In each case, the organization allows one particular issue to dominate within the theme of the woman protagonist's struggle for power: in *Barren Ground,* Dorinda struggles to take control over nature; in *Their Eyes Were Watching God,* Janie's primary struggle is with language; in *The Optimist's Daughter,* mastery over time, which succeeds only when one understands time's grip on human relationships, is Laurel's challenge. Nature, language, and time are male domains as these writers define them at the outset of their works. Men, not women, farm in *Barren Ground;* men, not women, speak in their big voices in *Their Eyes Were Watching God;* the father, not the daughter, winds the clock in *The Optimist's Daughter.* All this, of course, is what must change. For each woman character, taking possession—of nature, language, or time—means taking possession of self, a first act of creation. This is the story that these creating women tell.

Rituals of Sowing and Reaping: Dorinda Oakley's Work

Barren Ground follows Dorinda Oakley first through her young girlhood, as she falls in love with Dr. Jason Greylock, becomes pregnant, finds that her lover has married someone else, and moves to New York, where she has a miscarriage. In a second section, she returns to Virginia where we witness her struggle to restore her family's weed-choked farm and her own wounded psyche. After her parents' deaths, Dorinda marries a widower, Nathan Pedlar, with the understanding that there will be no sexual intimacy in their relationship. As a couple, the two farm their land wisely and diligently, earning enough from Dorinda's place, Old Farm, to purchase Jason Greylock's neglected estate, Five Oaks, when he loses all he owns through mismanagement and alcoholism. In the third and last section, Dorinda works with obsessive energy to reclaim Jason's lands. Now, as a maturing woman, she begins to find a meaning for her life beyond the bitterness and revenge that had been her driving emotions. The book's three sections are given similar symbolic titles from nature. Each names a form of useless, wasted vegetation which grows in the barren Virginia soil: "Broomsedge," "Pine," and "Life-Everlasting." Dorinda's life and her restored lands move in counter-direction to the seemingly inevitable cycles of natural decay that these section headings announce. In this way, Glasgow charts Dorinda's determined movement away from the fate that would be considered natural for her. Jason, as Glasgow says in *A Certain Measure,* "surrendered through inherited weakness" to "the slow seasons, the blighted crops, the long droughts, the sudden frosts,—all this impotence of nature" (161). Dorinda finds the will to survive in fighting this "impotence of nature," reflected in the land's useless outgrowths—the broomsedge, pine, and life-everlasting. She lives to change nature, proving herself in "work which . . . created anew the surroundings amid which she lived" (*BG* 337).

When we first see Dorinda with her "April face" and orange shawl, she seems to contradict the barrenness of the winter world around her. Yet, like it, she is trapped in physical processes. We meet her just as she has felt her first stirrings of sexual attraction for young Doctor Greylock, who has returned to Pedlar's Mill to care for his sick father. For Dorinda, meeting Jason made the world seem "as if an April flush had passed over the waste places" (13). Yet Dorinda's father and her friend Rose Emily are also slowly dying; the actual season is not spring but winter; the dreary land is blanketed with snow. Dorinda's world, in spite of her own youth and awakened sexuality, is trapped in decay. As her romance proceeds, she seems "transformed": her "immature beauty bloomed and ripened into its summer splendour" just as the season itself was ripening. Love, however, does not make her stronger but only more vulnerable. As she surrenders to feelings, Dorinda loses both strength and reality. "If the natural Dorinda still survived beneath this unreal Dorinda, she was visible only in momentary sparkles of energy" (107), Glasgow comments. The most significant transformation is Dorinda's loss of her voice, her unique mind and selfhood. Glasgow describes how Dorinda sits in "ecstatic dumbness" with her lover; "feeling . . . had drugged her until only half of her being was awake" (107). Love, like nature itself, is a force which does not promote but instead diminishes individual human strength. Barrenness results when the land surrenders to nature in Dorinda's environment; likewise barrenness is the consequence of surrendering to love in her personal life. Her struggle against barrenness, as Glasgow defines it, must also be a struggle against both nature and romantic love.

Dorinda's love for Jason has the same effect as her father's attachment to the land: "he had known nothing but toil," Glasgow tells us; "he had no language but the language of toil" (115). Both Dorinda and her father are made "dumb" by an enslavement to lives governed by physical responses. The Oakley farm epitomizes nature's innate barrenness: "They owned a thousand acres of scrub pine, scrub oak, and broomsedge, where a single cultivated corner was like a solitary island in some chaotic sea" (7). Joshua Oakley, we are told, had been "all his life . . . a slave to the land, harnessed to the elemental forces, struggling inarticulately against the blight of poverty and the barrenness of the soil" (40).

The first section of *Barren Ground* links Dorinda's dreams of escape and romance, symbolized by her love for Jason, to her reality, symbolized by her family's barren farm and her parents' monotonous life of endless toil. She has a premonition that "she and her parents were products of the soil as veritably as were the scant crops and the exuberant broomsedge" (125). If this is true, then nature in the form of her passion for Jason will defeat her as it has defeated her father. The patriarchal system that he, along with his community, accepts, dominated by limiting traditions and a philosophy of surrender to nature, is a dying world that can take Dorinda down with it.

Jason's betrayal, while it destroys the dream of her youth, nevertheless allows Dorinda to escape the broomsedge, which "was not only wild stuff, but a kind of fate" (113). Self-exiled in New York, she learns a new meaning for home. In her mind, she can see Old Farm, "the fields, the road, the white gate, the long low house, the lamp shining in the front window." The memory of home, as opposed to the reality, brings her back to life, releasing "some imprisoned force in the depths of her being" (239). At this point, she begins to read books on dairy farming, in order to learn how to take back the land from nature. In her description of Dorinda's mental labors, Glasgow appropriates images of farming: "When Dr. Burch arranged for the course of lectures, she attended them regularly, adding, with diligence, whatever she could to her knowledge of methods; gleaning, winnowing, storing away in her memory the facts which she thought might some day be useful. Before her always were the neglected fields" (240–41). Dorinda's mastery of the land represents the mind's mastery of matter. When she makes the decision to return to Old Farm, saying, "I belong to the abandoned fields" (245), she speaks not as one who plans to surrender but as one who plans to conquer.

When Dorinda returns to Old Farm to begin her reclamation, her father is dying. The world that is to be transformed becomes, at this point, a woman's world. The land belongs to, in fact is returned to, woman's hands, for it had actually been Dorinda's mother's inheritance from her grandfather.[3] Dorinda's relationship with her mother symbolizes the daughter's transformation: she inherits her mother's domain yet avoids her hopeless fate. We read that fate in the older woman's face, which "was as parched and ravaged as the drought-stricken landscape" (117). Dorinda has a continual struggle to avoid becoming the kind of woman her mother was, the kind of woman that her community would expect her to be as well. Mrs. Oakley's life becomes an illustration of one of the historical facts that Glasgow supplies for this Virginia country at the beginning of the novel: "The old men stayed by the farms, and their daughters withered dutifully beside them" (5). She has sacrificed herself for her husband and sons with a "morbid unselfishness" that Dorinda comes to see as "the greatest cross in her life" (45). Her advice to Dorinda, to "make up your mind that whatever happens, you ain't going to let any man spoil your life," is advice that Mrs. Oakley could not follow herself (104). The mother, unlike the father, exhibits a kind of indomitable strength, yet she exists only through nervous energy, with no vision other than duty and custom to sustain her. She casts a blighting shadow on her daughter's plans when she says, "In my time, I've watched many a big bloom that brought forth mighty small fruit" (266). Her tone and imagery express her own denial of fertility, the mother's gift of creativity stifled. Thus, while Dorinda respects her mother's energy, she recognizes a futility that threatens her own life as well; there were times, Glasgow tells us, "that she could not breathe within the stark limitations of her mother's point of view" (298). Mrs. Oakley raises three children, while Dorinda conceives only once and loses the child in a miscarriage. By her society's standards, then, Dorinda would seem to be the barren one, yet Glasgow makes clear that the greater creativity belongs to the childless daughter. Of the mother, we learn finally, "dying was the happiest part of her life" (333), for in her illness "her marriage and motherhood vanished from her memory" (334).

When Dorinda leaves her home for New York, she is pregnant, though unmarried. Her experience with Jason makes the thought of a sexual relationship repugnant; after her first tragic venture, and with her mother's unhappy example before her, she must find some other creative outlet for herself. Significantly, the scene in which she begins to think about how she might make Old Farm into a productive dairy takes place in her employer's nursery, where Mrs. Faraday is nursing her baby. Here Mrs. Faraday warns that her plan "would be drudgery, even if you succeeded, and you ought not to look forward to that. You ought to marry, my dear" (243). In this most maternal of all settings, Glasgow juxtaposes two opposite choices, yet also suggests that Dorinda's dairy represents a path that could be as fulfilling and creative as Mrs. Faraday's. An important question for the novel concerns Dorinda's fertility and her femininity in relation to her rejection of marriage, her preference for a commitment to what is clearly defined as man's business. Has she been so psychologically damaged by Jason's betrayal that she must totally repress the "womanly" side in her nature in rejecting the sexual option for her body? Must she become "mannish" or unfeminine in order to complete a vision of herself as an autonomous human being? When she dons overalls to go out to milk her cows, is she expressing her desire to be a man, or at least to deny that she is a woman?

To answer these questions, we need to listen to Dorinda's voice. When she goes to her neighbor's farm to buy his cows, she looks at his bull "with admiration and envy, while he returned her look with royal, inscrutable eyes." Yet what she thinks reveals something different from the desire to be male: "I wonder if I shall ever own a creature like that?" And aloud, she comments, "He looks as if he owned everything and yet despised it" (286). The goal of ownership, not maleness, is what drives Dorinda. She wears overalls in connection with work that is still explicitly female, milking the cows that she wants to be "handled properly." Thus her clothes are an assertion of freedom, not masculinity. When she takes over Old Farm, she turns the overplowed and useless land into pasture. Ploughing, with its connotations of the male's relationship to women as well as earth, is replaced by milking, with its connotations of female nourishment. Dorinda's rejection of physical relationships with men, then, can be seen not as a rejection or denial of her identity as woman but as a rejection of the degradation and dependency that she experienced in her affair with Jason. For her, self-ownership supplants the goal of marriage which, in her community, means a total sacrifice of self.

The creative potential that Dorinda realizes is best represented by the connections that she reestablishes with the earth over the long period that follows her return home. After her father's funeral, she begins to feel restored emotionally to herself. The death of her father frees her from one cause of her emotional barrenness—the patriarchal ordering that gave him authority to regulate the means of creation on his farm, an authority for which he was temperamentally unfit. Dorinda replaces her subordinate relationship to her father with a "kinship" relationship to the land: Glasgow writes, "Kinship with the land was filtering through her blood into her brain; and she knew that this transfigured instinct was blended of pity, memory, and passion. Dimly she felt that only through this fresh emotion could she attain permanent liberation of spirit" (299). A sense of connectedness with the land, then, for Dorinda means a re-integration with a lost part of herself that is liberated when she begins to recognize her own emotions—pity and passion—long buried away from memory. In *A Certain Measure,* Glasgow argues that the novel's theme of "the reclamation of the farm" had been "over-emphasized" by some critics; for her, it was "merely an episode," important for what it could tell, symbolically, about Dorinda's inner nature. What mattered most, Glasgow explained, was that Dorinda "would never lose her inner fidelity, that vital affirmation of life, 'I think, I feel, I am'" (*CM* 160). In the last section of *Barren Ground,* the successful process of giving life to the land begins to carry over into Dorinda's inner life. Recognizing "kinship with the land" means healing the division of mind, feeling, and being within herself.

For many years after her homecoming, Dorinda felt as though part of her were dead; her sense of betrayal and futility cast a shadow over every forward step. As she watched her mother's slow dying, she visu-alized her own living death, asking, "Would nothing thaw the frozen lake that enveloped her being? Would she never again become living and human?" (331). We see that Dorinda can indeed "suffer acutely," as "she longed with all her soul" to do, for her mother's pain hurts her deeply. Yet she denies her own compassion and involvement because feeling and failure are too deeply linked in her experience of what it means to be human. The question that Glasgow forces Dorinda to ask, in one of the many scenes that bring out her vital mental life, defines the novel's direction: "was it simply that feeling like hers never died, that it returned again and again, in some changed form, to the place where it had first taken root?" (384). This cyclic return of feeling marks Dorinda's whole history, yet she does not acknowledge it until death forces a final confrontation.

Dorinda's story, in its final phase, shows her connections to Demeter and Persephone as two related, separated, cyclically dispersed sides of her own being. Her return to Virginia is a return both to life and to death. During her thirties and forties, she presides over the rebirth of the land, wielding authority "as imperiously as a king who refuses to abdicate" (397). Once Old Farm is successfully established as a dairy, she turns to Five Oaks, the place that would have been her home had Jason married her: "Only by giving herself completely, only by enriching the land with her abundant vitality, could she hope to restore the farm. Reclaiming the abandoned fields had become less a reasonable purpose than a devouring passion in her mind and heart" (397). The language here is Demeter's language; enriching, restoring, reclaiming, vitality, passion are the attributes of the Grain Mother herself. Yet Dorinda during these years also presides over four funerals: her father's, her mother's, her husband, Nathan Pedlar's, and Jason Greylock's. So her links to Demeter are matched by links to the concept of Persephone as Queen of the Underworld, a world of death and defeat. Beyond Virginia, the outer world, too, is caught up in wasteful slaughter, as World War I runs its course. Dorinda's response to the faraway war is revealing: "Only when she saw victory in terms of crops, not battles, could she feel that she was part of it. . . . That men should destroy one another appeared to her less incredible than that they should deliberately destroy the resources which made life endurable" (446). If her response seems callous, we can reflect that the key factors in Dorinda's interest are womanly and nurturing; war is man's way of death while crops are woman's way of life. Yet the death of Jason Greylock brings her face to face, finally, with her own psychic death, touching her in a way that even the deaths of parents and husband never did.

The symbolic value of Jason, who consistently has more reality in Dorinda's imagination than as a flesh-and-blood man, lies in his associations with Death. He first appears in winter snow; when he visits Dorinda's friend Rose Emily, he brings only the stark message that she is dying; his frail, deranged wife dreams that she bears children whom he drowns, and she finally drowns herself. In a symbolic sense, Dorinda's obsession with Jason, the revenge that motivates so many of her actions throughout the course of her story, represents her lifelong struggle with Death, a Demeter struggle, we might say, that continually renews her.

In the novel's finale, Dorinda must deal with Death's most ironic victory: Jason himself dies and leaves her without the adversary who has defined her struggle. Before she ever returned to Pedlar's Mill, Dorinda had dreamed of plowing a field of thistles. Each thistle, in the dream, carried Jason's face in its center, "millions of purple flaunting heads" springing up faster than she can plough them under (240). Her resolve, "I am going to plough them under, if it kills me," expresses the crux of her relationship with Jason—it is not only woman vs. man, or, within herself, hate vs. love, but life vs. death. When Dorinda agrees to take the dying Jason to her home, preparing his room almost as though it were a nursery, birth and death and the meaning of her life as a woman come together. Her role changes from rejected lover or revengeful adversary to protectress and nurse; in his illness, Jason becomes a child, someone, at last, who "was dependent upon her compassion" (500). The despair that she feels when he dies has a great deal more to do with her craving for life than with revenge. In his death, he confronts her with the pain of living as a whole human being.

Glasgow shaped the ending of *Barren Ground* to affirm not resignation, a settling for less than life, but self-awareness, an acceptance of the cyclic nature of life, which will bring love and betrayal, success and failure, all in turn. The final scene, in which Dorinda awakens to a new feeling of hope after a night of despair, is one that has occurred many times in the story. The imagery places her on the verge of renewal: Dorinda bathes at sunrise, goes out to find the earth smelling of dawn, and discovers, as she has many times before, her connections to the land. Again, the symbolism of this connection is important: "The spirit of the land was flowing into her, and her own spirit, strengthened and refreshed, was flowing out again toward life. This was the permanent self, she knew" (509). What the land represents, here more clearly for Dorinda than at any time earlier, is her own life. Her life, like the land, is an adversary as well as a sustaining force; moreover, it is always changing, always hungering, always demanding. A permanent self is a connected self, one active with opposing needs, and not a "finished" self, which is why she smiles so ironically when she says, once more, "I've finished with all that" (511). The scene, in which an autumn dawn holds in tension beginnings and endings, speaks of cycles—Dorinda will never be finished. "While the soil endured," she thinks, "while the seasons bloomed and dropped, while the ancient, beneficent ritual of sowing and reaping moved in the fields, she knew that she could never despair of contentment" (509–10). All the oppositions of this final perception are Dorinda's own inner oppositions, the source of her creativity and her permanent, never-finished self.

Pulling in the Horizon: Janie Crawford's Voice

Their Eyes Were Watching God presents a woman character, Janie Craw-ford, whose journey to creative selfhood is conceived in similar terms to Dorinda's in *Barren Ground*. Both enter their fertile years with romantic visions tying happiness and self-completion to sexual fulfillment. When Dorinda sees Jason, "the whole of life [blossoms] out like a flower in the sun" (12). In young Janie's situation, a seductive vision accompanies her discovery of her sexuality; she sees "a dust-bearing bee sink into the sanctum of a bloom," which for her explains the mystery of sexual union in marriage. In her yearning for this encounter, she wishes to be only "*any* tree in bloom! With kissing bees singing of the beginning of the world" (24–25). The illusion of romance is presented in both works as a blend of biological and cultural determinism binding women to men and to sexual definitions of themselves.

Like Dorinda's mother, Janie's grandmother offers no alternative vision to supplant her culture's decree for women: servitude and diminish-ment. The grandmother, in marrying sixteen-year-old Janie to a wealthy, much older man, argues that "Heah you got uh prop tuh lean on all yo' bawn days, and big protection" (41), the best a woman, in particular a black woman, can hope for. She was the kind of person, Janie thinks, who "loved to deal in scraps. Here Nanny had taken the biggest thing God ever made, the horizon . . . and pinched it in to such a little bit of a thing that she could tie it about her granddaughter's neck tight enough to choke her. She hated the old woman who had twisted her so in the name of love" (138). Janie and Dorinda seek horizons; Dorinda's "gaze was on the horizon," Glasgow tells us (289), while Hurston tells us, in her final image of Janie, that "she pulled in her horizon like a great fish-net" (286). But the women who raised Janie and Dorinda closed down the daughters' visions of both self and world. Thus they represent entrapment more than nurture, the death of dreams more than survival. The versions of motherhood that they offer, lives of toil, sacrifice, and disillusion, do much to explain why their daughters never become mothers. Janie marries three times, but like Dorinda, she never bears children. As if to announce another departure from mothers' traditions, both women wear overalls, not to disguise or deny their femininity, but in order to free themselves from what women's clothes represent—limits on movement, on vocation, on possibilities. Janie enjoys a completely satisfying sexual relationship in her last marriage, to Tea Cake. She finds her own voice, however, only when she returns to her house alone, like Dorinda, to become the sole owner of both home and self.

Janie and Dorinda look younger than the women around them who have lived supposedly more "womanly" lives. More important, once they separate themselves from men's controlling definitions, they begin to become creators. Both of these novels rely on imagery from nature to indicate their woman character's interior differences. The predominantly rural settings highlight weather, seasons, growing plants, the smell of soil, and animal health. Both women time their lives in rhythms of work that are seasonal, cyclical; they are planters, food-bringers, gardeners. When Janie leaves the Everglades after Tea Cake's death, she carries away only one thing: "a package of garden seed that Tea Cake had bought to plant," which she puts "in her breast pocket" so that she can "plant them for remembrance" when she returns home (283). Yet while Dorinda's struggle is defined primarily in terms of her symbolic associations with nature, in *Their Eyes Were Watching God* Janie's growth into creating womanhood gains another dimension through Hurston's handling of language and voice. Progressively growing into selfhood through her three marriages, Janie achieves a voice that provides her story's unifying frame, testifying to a woman's mastery of language as well as to the wholeness of the woman whose story we hear.

Their Eyes Were Watching God opens with a detached voice that offers, as its first observation, a distinction between the ways that men and women dream: men passively wait for their dreams to "come in with the tide" or to "sail forever on the horizon"; on the other hand, women, more actively responsive to their own visions, make their dreams "the truth" by their capacities for remembering or forgetting and then "act and do things accordingly" (9). This narrator begins by remembering one particular woman, then acts upon this memory by telling her story. The woman at "the beginning of this" is a Demeter figure who "had come back from burying the dead." She is wearing overalls but is hardly unfeminine; the overalls do not hide "firm buttocks like she had grape fruits in her hip pockets" and "pugnacious breasts trying to bore holes in her shirt" (11). The woman is Janie, who had left the small town of Eatonville years earlier as a rich widow chasing a "no 'count" younger man, or so the townsfolk would say. Yet the voice we hear belongs not to any of the "porchsitters" who watch her return, ready to sit in judgment. This narrative voice instead will belong by story's end (an end which comes around to this beginning) both to Janie and to other women who feel called to retell her story.

The opening narrator of *Their Eyes Were Watching God* is an omniscient one capable of blending the talk of the community with the thoughts of the woman who is their "subject." The power of this voice is absolute, controlling nature ("the sun was gone, but he had left his footprints in the sky"), time ("It was the time to hear things and talk"), and the speech of others ("These sitters had been tongueless, earless, eyeless conveniences all day long") (10). As Janie enters the scene, her presence summoned by the voice that she will make her own, the other "tongueless" sitters, the gossips of Eatonville, are summoned too, as witnesses, contributors to her story. Their comments, however, have only the force of "words walking without masters; walking altogether like harmony in a song" (10). Janie, not the porchsitters, is designated as the master of words, theirs as well as hers, which she will blend as the teller of the tale that encloses them all. The cruelty that they want to inflict through their words results from what they see as Janie's greatest wrongdoing: "she didn't stop and tell us all her business" (13), as her friend Pheoby remarks. When Janie had left Eatonville with Tea Cake years earlier, she had not yet found herself, so she could not then have created the story that she will now "stop and tell." She warns Pheoby, who brings a food offering to the newly returned traveller, "Ah ain't brought home a thing but mahself" (14); yet that, as Pheoby replies, is "a gracious plenty," what Janie lacked before and all that a storyteller needs.

In this prelude to the chronological narrative of Janie's life, the bodiless voice moves through the "tongueless" community to Janie through her friend Pheoby, a listener who "feeds" the story by her interest and, as audience, provides a new community that can hear and then retell. Janie will instruct Pheoby, who has offered to return to the porchsitters and "tell 'em what you tell me to tell 'em" (17). In talking to Pheoby, Janie makes knowledge the prerequisite to telling a story: "people like dem wastes up too much time puttin' they mouf on things they don't know nothin' about" (17), she says, while she herself has been to "de big convention of livin'" (18) so that she has earned the right to be talker and teller.[4] To explain why she has returned to Eatonville, Janie tells Pheoby that "Tea Cake is gone" (18). Pheoby's reply is one that even we who "know" the story on one level might also make; she says, "It's hard for me to understand" (19). Janie must then begin again, since, as she says, "'tain't no use in me telling you somethin' unless Ah give you de understandin' to go 'long wid it" (19). Consequently, the telling that follows accomplishes two goals at once: it teaches understanding to an initiate storyteller (Pheoby) while it also satisfies, for the teacher (Janie), "that oldest human longing—self revelation" (18). The story is her journey to the self that she is now able to reveal. In what follows, then, she creates the three elements of narrative: a self, self-knowledge, and a new, knowledgeable narrator. Janie as creating character thus establishes herself as a powerful controlling agent through a voice that transforms experience into words, words into story, and story into meaning.

Hurston's title, *Their Eyes Were Watching God*, refers to the way that people look to a higher power to explain why things happen. The phrase appears in the story when Janie, Tea Cake, and their friends who work the bean fields are trapped in the Everglades during a hurricane. As they huddle in their shanty during the storm, Janie and Tea Cake watch the door, "their eyes straining against crude walls and their souls asking if He meant to measure their puny might against His. They seemed to be staring at the dark, but their eyes were watching God" (236). They are looking to God for meaning in this awful exhibit of His power, much as Pheoby looks to Janie when she returns mysteriously to Eatonville. In the prelude to her own story, Janie is designated as one with the all-knowing power of revelation, the one against whom other storytellers must measure their might, the one who can talk up her own kind of storm.

The language and dialects of the opening scene vary considerably as we move around among tellers and talkers, yet one kind of language stands out, particularly in Janie's dialogue with Pheoby. Both women, but especially Janie, flavor the conversation with folk maxims, tight, funny aphorisms that are a species of black American mother wit.[5] Virtually every comment that Janie makes in this section is accompanied by what Karla Holloway calls "adornment": "Ah ain't had a thing on mah stomach today exceptin' mah hand"; "you switches a mean fanny around a kitchen"; "they's a lost ball in de high grass"; "They don't know if life is a mess of corn-meal dumplings, and if love is a bed-quilt"; "unless you see de fur, a mink skin ain't no different from a coon hide." Words work here to accomplish meaning in an especially appropriate way. Holloway, in her study of Hurston's language, writes that "Hurston's fiction speaks of the primacy of the word. . . . Within the text, the affirmative power invested in this word is an affirmation of black self. Dialect carries the poetry of myth in its adorned structure, and when dialect and narrative voices merge to each carry poetry, they each celebrate the poetic artisan" (114–15). In this way, Holloway believes, "Hurston . . . celebrated herself through her word, crafted herself, affirmed herself, and perhaps most important and most primal, *named* herself." By giving the mature, story-framing Janie a dialect which "carries the poetry of myth in its adorned structure," as these examples show, her character likewise celebrates, crafts, and names herself. Because the young Janie whom we meet within the narrative proper has not acquired this language, the novel becomes a study of the process whereby she achieves the powerful capacities that we hear in the frame.

Hurston begins chapter 2, the narrative "proper," with Janie speaking in first person about her early years. Janie reveals a childhood self that had no knowledge of its being. The little girl we meet has no name; she is called "Alphabet" because "people had done named me different names" (21). She does not know her race until she is shown a photograph of herself standing with her white employer's children. "Ah couldn't recognize dat dark chile as me," Janie tells Pheoby. As Janie proceeds with the story, "in soft, easy phrases" (23), Hurston changes to a third-person narration to better distinguish the older, knowing Janie from the girl who has few words to capture her early experience of love. When Janie speaks to her grandmother in this section, her words are halting, simple, "unadorned." When she tries to argue against her grandmother's demand that she marry old Logan Killicks, her one metaphor, "He look like some old skull-head in de grave yard" (28), results in a violent retort from the old woman who fears that her granddaughter will end up with a man "usin' yo' body to wipe his foots on" (27). Consequently, Janie retreats into silence, while her grandmother's voice begins "snagging on the prongs of her feelings" as she tells Janie her own history, a story of all black women's oppression.

Janie's grandmother immediately names a kind of nonbeing for both herself and her granddaughter as she explains what she sees as their position in the world: "Honey, de white man is de ruler of everything as fur as Ah been able tuh find out. . . . So de white man throw down de load and tell de nigger man tuh pick it up. He pick it up because he have to, but he don't tote it. He hand it to his womenfolks. De nigger woman is de mule uh de world so fur as Ah can see" (29). Woman as mule, Nanny's primary metaphor, dehumanizes and unnames black women. By inserting the grandmother's story of her struggles as a slave into this section, Hurston gives a kind of stark counterpoint to the direction that Janie's own quest will take. Nanny's story is a slave narrative without the sense of ultimate liberating of self that a narrative like Harriet Jacobs's was designed to illustrate. "Ah didn't want to be used for a work-ox and a brood-sow and Ah didn't want mah daughter used dat way neither" (31), she insists, as Jacobs might have. Instead she had dreams that she might one day "preach a great sermon about colored women sittin' on high." Nanny actually summoned the courage to run away from her master's plantation when her mistress beat her and threatened to sell her daughter because the baby was its master's child. Yet when the daughter, for whom she had great dreams, was raped, Nanny gave in to the oppressor's own view that black women had no right to dream of "sittin' on high." Her fear for Janie, that "menfolks white or black" might make "a spit cup outa you" (37), cancels her hope that Janie would someday "take a stand on high ground lak Ah dreamed" (32). Her lesson to Janie is that "Neither can you stand alone by yo'self" (31). Nanny cannot see that the "protection" she arranges for Janie in the marriage to

Killicks is only another name for the slavery that she had once fought so hard to escape.

Janie emphatically denies this legacy. After her second husband, Joe Starks, dies, she retells her grandmother's story to Pheoby in a language far different from the kind that the grandmother herself used. The knowledge that Janie gained in her two unhappy marriages, both of which made her men's objects instead of a woman standing for herself, allows her to give a changed reading of Nanny's story: "She was borned in slavery time when folks, dat is black folks, didn't sit down anytime dey felt lak it. So sittin' on porches lak de white madam looked lak a mighty fine thing tuh her. . . . but Pheoby, Ah done nearly languished tuh death up dere. Ah felt like de world wuz cryin' extry and Ah ain't read de common news yet" (172). Janie shows here that she is learning to "read" by the light of her own experience so that she can reach the stage, telling informed by understanding, that she offers to Pheoby in the opening frame. First, however, she must find a way to speak consistently her own words in her own voice.

During her first two marriages, when Janie realizes that her husbands expect her to give up her voice to enhance theirs, she reaches for a new language as a way to escape: "new words would have to be made," she thinks when she leaves Logan Killicks, and when her marriage to Joe Starks dissolves, she reasons, "So new thoughts had to be thought and new words said" (55, 125). There are times during her marriage to Joe that she speaks out, trying to counter his insults with assertions that "womenfolks thinks sometimes too" (110–11). Yet "gradually, she pressed her teeth together and learned to hush" (111), until Joe, in effect, rapes her with his words. One of his cutting remarks to her "was like somebody snatched off part of a woman's clothes while she wasn't looking" (121). In responding, Janie is fighting for her life: "Talkin' 'bout me lookin' old!'," she retorts. "When you pull down yo' britches, you look lak de change uh life" (123). With these words Janie transforms herself, enacting her own very different "change of life" and one which emasculates her husband, whose virility has depended on her silent submission. His voice is turned back upon him with devastating results. Later, when Joe lies dying, Janie drives the point home: "Too busy listening tuh yo' own big voice," she tells him in her own new voice (133).

With Joe Starks, Janie's silence was forced and her voice usually unnatural. When she finally spoke, her language came from the menfolk's arsenal. With Tea Cake, Janie finds new areas and new functions for both voicing and silence. The change is illustrated by the new location for storytelling that she finds after she marries Tea Cake. In the novel's second section, when Janie was Mrs. Starks, the men told stories on the store porch, usually stories about women or mules (symbolically the same thing, in the lexicon Nanny learned from male oppressors). No one was more at home on the porch than Joe Starks, who in his "high chair" there dominated the storytelling sessions. Janie "loved the conversation and sometimes she thought up good stories," but "Joe had forbidden her to indulge" (85). When she marries Tea Cake, the storytelling moves inside, into Janie's—woman's—domain. We learn that this house "was full of people every night . . . ; some came to talk and tell stories, but most of them came to get into whatever game was going on or might go on" (199–200). Significantly, storytelling and gambling go hand in hand in Janie's and Tea Cake's home. The gambling is for Tea Cake, the stories for Janie: "The men held big arguments here like they used to do on the store porch. Only here, she could listen and laugh and even talk some herself if she wanted to. She got so she could tell big stories herself from listening to the rest" (200). Janie's transformation from silent object into connecting subject is dramatically established in this description. She is now not either listener or speaker, but both.

Janie's increasing freedom, her growth into personhood, can be measured by her ability to join in the stories, yet stories raise risks as well. To enter Tea Cake's world on equal terms is to encounter the potentially violent side of both love and living; Janie's love is once described as "self-crushing" (192). Tea Cake at one point beats Janie, "no brutal beating at all," just one that "reassured him in possession" (218). Janie's submission to Tea Cake's beating demonstrates that, while she has learned how to speak, she has not yet taken possession of herself. Janie acquiesces to Tea Cake's gambling with their lives when the hurricane comes; at this point, their relationship's risks become a palpable force. A mad dog bites Tea Cake while they are caught in the storm. Several weeks later, Tea Cake, maddened by rabies, tries to shoot Janie. She is forced to kill or be killed, her "sacrificing self" trapped into shooting the man who had given her "the chance for loving service" (273). While the circumstances differ, Tea Cake's attack places Janie in the same situation which led her to hurl her devastating insult at Joe Starks. Both men demand possession —Joe as a form of power, Tea Cake as a form of love—which sentences Janie to silence, a kind of death. Only after Tea Cake dies does an original storytelling role begin for Janie. While she lived to serve men, they controlled her story.

When Janie is tried for Tea Cake's murder, she once more, as with Joe Starks, has to fight for her life by seizing words in her own defense. This time, in the courtroom, language becomes an issue of both race and gender. The "colored folk" come "with their tongues cocked and loaded, the only real weapon left to weak folks. The only killing tool they are allowed to use in the presence of white folks" (275). In this instance, their tongues, associated with maleness, are aimed against Janie, who finds protection in identifying, for the first time, with women. When she sees a group of wealthy white women who come to watch her trial, Janie at first feels separate: "What need had *they* to leave their richness to come look on Janie in her overalls?" (275). Yet she senses an instinctive sympathy, one that transcends race or class. Unlike the men, these women "didn't seem too mad" (a word associating all these men with Tea Cake's fatal madness). Recognizing their difference, Janie longs to make women the audience for her story, thinking, "It would be nice if she could make *them* know how it was instead of those menfolks" (275). The black men convict Janie of two sexual transgressions: she put her own life above Tea Cake's, and at the trial, she tells her own story. Both acts threaten their manhood: Janie should have sacrificed herself for her man, and for them, they think. When Janie is called to the stand, we see her voice take on its essential function: self-defense, in the largest sense. Janie "sat there and told and when she was through she hushed" (278), her quiet voice a contrast to the "tongue storm" which "struck the Negroes like wind among palm trees" (276). When she finishes and the jury finds her not guilty, the words, "So she was free" (279), indicate several levels of release. She is free to speak, to possess herself, and to identify herself as a woman, a position which gives her new power, since her women listeners "stood around her like a protecting wall" (280) after her acquittal.

The courtroom scene, where everyone "leaned over to listen while she talked," frees Janie for a specifically woman's kind of storytelling. In the novel's last two pages, we are returned to the frame, where Janie, sitting on the porch of her house, finishes the story that freed her in the courtroom and brought her home to herself. Pheoby's response, "Ah done growed ten feet higher from jus' listenin' tuh you" (284), shows that she is prepared to take the story as her own and retell it with empowered understanding. The "finished silence" that the women share testifies to their control over the timing and placing of voice. Teller and listener, they have brought a new self into being.

Hurston, like Glasgow in *Barren Ground,* closes *Their Eyes Were Watching God* with a scene in which natural change signifies a woman's growth into creative selfhood. Whereas, in *Barren Ground,* Dorinda awakens refreshed at dawn, in *Their Eyes Were Watching God,* Janie sits on the porch of her house, watching dusk turn to dark before she climbs the stairs to find refreshing sleep in a room of her own. The images of light and rising in the novel's last scene are the substance of myth: "Janie mounted the stairs with her lamp. The light in her hand was like a spark of sun-stuff washing her face in fire. Her shadow behind fell black and headlong down the stairs" (285). Men might watch with resignation as their dreams "sail forever on the horizon," as we are told in the first paragraph of the novel, but Janie, in the last paragraph, "pulled in her horizon like a great fish-net. Pulled it from around the waist of the world and draped it over her shoulder. So much of life in its meshes! She called in her soul to come and see" (286).

Their Eyes Were Watching God has been called "A Portrait of the Artist as a Young Black Woman,"[6] a description that is borne out by the images of Janie as light-bringer and caller of souls as well as by the voice that she claims for her story. The novel both traces the process and celebrates the result of Janie's artistic empowerment. When Janie tells Pheoby at the end, "you got tuh *go* there tuh *know* there. Yo' papa and yo' mama and nobody else can't tell yuh and show yuh" (285), she announces a completed transformation of daughter into artist, freed from the past and from patriarchal tradition to "go," to "know," and then to show and tell in story.

Sewing New Patterns: Laurel McKelva's Freed Hands

We might assume that Laurel McKelva, in *The Optimist's Daughter,* has already completed the process of shaping self into artist that Janie's story traces. When we first meet Laurel, she has arrived in New Orleans to offer support to her father, who faces an operation for a detached retina. Laurel, too, faces her own crisis by having to deal with his new wife, Fay, a younger woman whose appalling selfishness and triviality make her the opposite of Laurel's deceased mother Becky. Laurel has evidently managed to put other crises behind her in the not too distant past: her mother's death after a terrible, debilitating illness and her husband's death during his service as a naval officer in World War II. Now a widow in her forties, Laurel is a survivor, an independent woman, and an artist. Even after her husband's and mother's deaths, she remained in Chicago, where she had moved many years before to study art. Her successful career as a fabric designer, her marriage, her full life far away from the family home in Mount Salus, Mississippi, would seem to indicate that Laurel, at the start of the novel, like Janie, at the end of her story, has finished a journey to self-knowledge and voice. Yet Laurel's experiences during her father's illness and after his death prove that her daughterhood was a position that she had never really left. She still has to "go there to know there," in Janie's words, and ironically, the "there" to which she must travel is her childhood home and her childhood memories of father and mother. While her parents, as Janie would say, can't tell or show Laurel what her life means, she finds that she has to start her journey away from them all over again in order to gain the knowledge she needs to live as a truly independent self and artist.

Laurel, like Dorinda and Janie, returns home not as a prodigal son might, seeking a blessing and reconciliation with the father, but as the daughter of Demeter, for whom the return home represents one portion of a cyclic journey. In *The Optimist's Daughter,* Laurel confronts parents, community, culture, and self with feelings that mix love, betrayal, hunger, and even hate. As "the optimist's daughter" of the title, Laurel is heir to her father's flawed vision. Thus her challenge is to become other than the optimist that her father was, for the optimist is one who tries to limit his vision to what he can control, rejecting what hurts, what changes, what dies. She must also become different from the daughter that both parents and community molded her to be, for the daughter is one who can live only in the past, defined by ideals that others choose for her. Laurel's challenge is to become fully an artist, one who both acknowledges the nature of life in time and accepts the past without being trapped in it. While Janie's task in *Their Eyes Were Watching God* was similar, Laurel's is framed not only by voice, an appropriation of language, but also by seeing, an appropriation of vision. The vision that becomes crucial for Laurel's return involves understanding how human relationships change in time and how she herself can be free to change without destroying what belongs to the past. This is the wisdom of Demeter and also the wisdom of memory, which becomes Laurel's ground for hope in *The Optimist's Daughter.*[7]

In "Some Notes on Time in Fiction," published in 1973 (a year after *The Optimist's Daughter* came out in novel form), Welty comments, "Man can feel love for place; he is prone to regard time as something of an enemy" (164). "Clock time," she adds, "has an arbitrary, bullying power over daily affairs that of course can't be gotten around" (165). Laurel's father at first optimistically tries to "get around," to accommodate or to deny this power, but when he at last comes face to face with old age, diminished strength, and loss of purpose, he finally gives himself over to time entirely. His response to the terminal illness of his first wife and his choice of a second wife indicate how far the optimist's viewpoint has driven him away from a clear vision of time's effects on the people and things that he values. Laurel, inheriting Judge McKelva's tendency for both accommodation and denial, comes dangerously close to losing herself to the same kind of despair that envelops her father after his eye operation. She finds a new perspective only when her return home for her father's funeral allows her, actually forces her, to see the complete pattern of her parents' lives together. She also must listen to all the voices of her childhood and hear, particularly in her mother's voice, questions from the past that can still threaten, but perhaps also redeem, her life in the present.

The questions that Laurel must ask operate as stages on an interior journey, one that reflects Demeter's search for a lost and buried part of herself in the depths of a world frozen in time. What did Fay, who insulted every value in her parents' world, really mean to her father? Why was Laurel herself, who had travelled so far away in years, miles, and perspective from her beginnings in Mount Salus, still no more than a long-lost child upon her return? What was the full story of her parents'

love for each other and of her own marriage to Phil Hand? The answers
to all of these questions offer not comfort but guilt, not reconciliation
with but separation from all that Laurel found valuable in the past. As
she takes up each question in turn, she travels to an underworld, an inner
world, of guilt and separation before discovering, in self-confrontation, a
way to accept the inevitable blunders of life that constitute change and
growth. In the novel's four sections Laurel moves through seasons of
change which loosen the grip that her father's view of the world has over
her life. She changes from the clock-watching, past-fearing daughter to
an artist who has discovered the power of memory over time. The settings for her revelations reflect the oppositional nature of her interior
journey. She travels from the "nowhere" of New Orleans to the tumul-
tuous and stifling "somewhere" of tiny Mount Salus. She moves, too,
from the interior of the family home, filled with cut flowers arranged to
memorialize her father, to her mother's garden, where weeds compete
for space with bulbs that must be separated and rose bushes that need
trimming. Still later, she moves from her father's library, with its high
windows, to her mother's sewing room, tucked darkly away off her parents' bedroom. Finally she moves from the "curtainless" kitchen where
she has one final confrontation with Fay to her "bridesmaids'" waiting
car, which will start her on her last journey to her own freed life in time.

Laurel arrives in New Orleans at Mardi Gras season, in Christian
ritual a time of revelry preceding a period of repentance and preparation for resurrection. Welty tells us that the suit that Laurel wore on
her trip from Chicago "was wintry for New Orleans" (3). Her clothes
suggest Persephone's journeying, but the symbolism is ambiguous—is
Laurel, in her trip to meet her father, leaving a frozen underworld or
returning to one? New Orleans from her window view in the hospital
is only a "nowhere . . . colorless and tarpatched"; even the river "was
not visible" to her there. Like her father she has problems with vision;
Fay asks her, when she finds Laurel asleep wearing her spectacles, with
a book in her lap, "Putting your eyes out too?" (25). With her father
Laurel seems in the grip of diminished sight and death, yet she is also
transformed, or returned, to a world that is thawing and blooming and
to her earlier identity as daughter. After his operation, her father, in
a "parched" voice, calls her "Polly," her childhood name. Through this

"slip," we see him turning away from Fay, who says herself that she belongs "to the future" (179), and back to what was behind him, people he loved but assumed he had lost to the past. Laurel will accompany him in this, his last journey.

In no way does Laurel seem more her father's daughter than in her obsession, during his postoperative days, with time. She frequently looks at her watch; in the pattern she establishes for her hospital visits, she begins Judge McKelva's day by telling him "what time her watch showed" (18), a comment that suggests other kinds of time that Laurel cannot reveal to him. "Time passing," we are told, was the force that "occupied his full mind," and Laurel feels a need to set "her inner chronology with his" (19). Both Laurel and her father look warily upon that "clock time" which, as Welty wrote in "Some Notes on Time in Fiction," was "something of an enemy." In New Orleans, time controls both daughter and father. The judge moves towards a death that he does not fight while Laurel is forced into "gearing herself to the time things took" (43). Yet Laurel will differ from her father in the response that she ultimately makes to time's thefts. Her father, we learn, had a horror of any "divergence from the affectionate and the real and the explainable and the recognizable" (146) which caused him, when his beloved Becky was dying, to become an optimist—to make himself willfully blind to truths he could not change. "When he reached a loss," his daughter remembers, "he simply put on his hat and went speechless out of the house to his office and worked for an hour or so getting up a brief for somebody" (146). What he could not control, in his man's way, he circumvented or denied. In New Orleans, his denial, his optimism, becomes an illness that he no longer has the strength to fight. Time, the enemy, wins because the judge cannot find an adequate vision with which to face what happens to life in time.

In Mount Salus, Judge McKelva had "done duty" by his parlor clock (73), keeping it running, controlling its passing by his own purposeful life. When Laurel returns to Mount Salus after his death, she discovers that the clock had stopped during his absence, as though his world had at last become impervious to the force of change, the will of the future. When Laurel "takes him home" to Mount Salus for his burial, she finds that she, too, is locked in a frame that does not seem to move forward. During the train journey from New Orleans to Mount Salus, she sees a gull "hanging with wings fixed, like a stopped clock on a wall" (45). Through this image, we are prepared for the way in which Laurel's life turns back to the past through the double event of her return home and her father's funeral. The train carrying father and daughter home is met by Laurel's "bridesmaids," her friends who for the moment have frozen themselves into the identity that her marriage and removal conferred. Time, then, seems to have stopped completely in a place where women accept back the living and the dead, where women keep the past and preside over the rituals that absorb human change.

One living reminder of Judge McKelva resists the Mount Salus rituals and women's ways of connecting present to past: his second wife, Fay Chisom. With her family (invited to the funeral by the only man who has a part in this drama, the blundering Major Bullock), Fay lets everyone know that rituals of remembrance and return do not stay time's hands completely. For Laurel, Fay is that part of her father that she most dreads and least understands. Welty tells us that "It was still incredible to Laurel," as she endured her stepmother's alien ways in New Orleans, "that her father, at nearly seventy, should have let anyone new, a beginner, walk in on his life" (26). Laurel's blindness to what Fay meant to her father is symptomatic of her own potentially fatal optimism. Fay quite simply represents change itself, which happens in time without even having to recognize time. For Judge McKelva, then, Fay offered another way around time, very different from Becky's way, but one which effectively delayed his confrontation with realities he did not want to accept. In committing himself, physically as well as socially, in marriage to Fay, Judge McKelva stepped briefly into an alliance which beat time at its own game. While to others she seemed a horror, desecrating the past, to him she represented life here and now, freed from the pain of the past. And, on her side, Fay attempted to keep her husband alive. When she "laid hands" on him in the hospital, as the angry nurse described it (32), she was trying "to scare him into living," "to make him quit his old-man foolishness" (175), she explains to Laurel. With her springlike green spike heels and her dangling green earrings, Fay could keep Judge McKelva from thinking (35) by immersing him in her purely physical energy. With no capacity for remembering or sharing emotion, Fay represents a kind of protection from memory itself.

The judge finally "sneaks out" on both Fay and Laurel, recognizing,

perhaps, the futility of both the past and the future in a present con-
sumed by pain. Yet Laurel and her women friends must still deal with
what her father knowingly brought into the world that they sought to
make safe for the past. Fay's brother runs a wrecking business; her
mother, who recognized that the McKelva home was "the very house to
hold a big funeral," recommends turning it into a boarding house (66,
96); Fay herself covered the mahogany headboard of Laurel's parents'
bed with "peach satin"—nothing of Laurel's past escapes Fay's changes,
not even the bed in which Laurel was born. Not surprisingly, it is Fay,
not Laurel, who "does business" with the undertaker. Fay's potentially
disastrous effect on the past that Mount Salus folks hold sacred shows
most clearly in her decision concerning where to bury Judge McKelva.
He is not to lie next to Becky, in a grave near a camellia bush that holds
"blooms living and dead," but in a new part of Mount Salus cemetery,
near the interstate, where "plastic poinsettias" mark new graves (90).
In this gesture, as in many others, Fay tells Laurel that her childhood
memories and her family's traditions are not safe from change. The
optimist's daughter, her bridesmaids, her father's "striking clock," her
mother's silver bells cannot meet change on its own "portable grass" turf,
the unthinking present, and survive unscathed. Only when Laurel turns
from the stepmother to the mother, reversing her father's direction, does
she find a means for making an effective challenge to time.

When Fay's mother tells Laurel that "you ain't got father, mother,
brother, sister, husband, chick, nor child" (69), she gives words to Laurel's undeniable alienation, which has kept her isolated for far longer
than Mrs. Chisom knows. The words of her mother's best friend, telling
her mildly that "daughters need to stay put, where they can keep a better
eye on us old folks" (61), are hardly less damning in their judgment.
When Fay, in New Orleans, created the lie that made her a Texas orphan
instead of one of a huge Chisom clan, she, too, hit Laurel close to home
in her fantasy: "After Papa died, we all gave up everything for Mama, of
course. Now that she's gone, I'm glad we did. Oh, I wouldn't have run
off and left anybody that needed me. Just to call myself an artist and
make a lot of money" (28). Fay, who was of course capable of doing just
that, can make Laurel feel like a betrayer, for Laurel has never recon-
ciled her daughter self with her artist self. Running off to call herself an

artist may have been an essential act of self-expression, but she, unlike Fay and very much like Welty herself, felt guilty for allowing herself to be, as Welty said in *One Writer's Beginnings,* the "loved one gone" (94). The return to Mount Salus brings her face to face with what both she and her father tried unsuccessfully to leave behind without accommodating: identities connecting them to people hurt and lost, who would even in death accuse them with their own hunger after life. Laurel's husband, her mother, and now even her father, in memory, rise up to make their loving accusations. Finding her mother's stories, remembering her mother's voice, gives Laurel at last a way to acknowledge their accusations and to make her own vulnerability into a victory over Fay.

Laurel finds her mother in two womanly, creative environments that restore her at last to herself: the garden outside and the sewing room inside her parents' home. On the day after the funeral, Laurel puts on an old pair of slacks and sweater to go outside to work in the iris bed behind her house. Like Dorinda's and Janie's overalls, these clothes reflect a liberating of identity, freedom not from femininity but from restraints against woman's full ability to move. While Laurel kneels in her mother's garden, her mother's friends sit with her, weaving stories of her parents' lives that remind her of her own. As she listens, "her mother's voice," a Demeter voice, "came back with each weed she reached for, and its name with it" (107). The wisdom that she can now take from her mother is a gardener's knowledge; as she envisions her mother saying, "That's how gardeners must learn to look at it," she also discovers that "Memory returned like spring. . . . Memory had the character of spring. In some cases, it was the old wood that did the blooming" (115). Her mother's gift was her understanding that natural processes sometimes took life forward, sometimes backward. It is a gift that Laurel recovers as she slowly begins to dig for memories that can keep the past creatively alive. When Laurel and her elderly company of women friends look at "Becky's Climber," a rose bush named for this master gardener, Laurel again hears her mother's voice, describing her efforts on behalf of the mysterious rose: Becky had boasted, "All I had to do was uncover it and give it the room it asked for. Look at it! It's on its own roots, of course, utterly strong" (114). This gardening wisdom is her bequest to her daughter, whom she had named for the state flower of West Virginia, her own long-lost home. Laurel must ask for her own room and find her own roots, her own strengths, in one last search through the home that she will soon lose.

In the room most closely connected with her mother, the sewing room, Laurel finds her roots in her mother's writing desk. Here Becky's saved letters, pictures, and souvenirs act, like the old ladies in the garden, to prompt Laurel's excavations of her past. What she finds in the sewing room are stories, just as when, a child, she had come to the room to hear the town's seamstress, Verna Longmeier, "sewing and making up tales or remembering all wrong what she saw and heard" (133). Her mother's writing desk provides Laurel with a chance to remember rightly the tales that hold the key to her identity. Coming back to the house just before a late night storm, Laurel is driven to the sewing room by her fear of a bird, a chimney swift, flying loose in the house. The sewing room is a small room off her parents' bedroom, Fay's room now and the one room that Laurel had not entered except to wake Fay on the morning of the funeral. Terrified of the bird, who strongly suggests her own hunger and entrapment, Laurel flees to her parents' room. Symbolically, she turns to her parents, to her secure role as daughter, to avoid knowledge of her own change. Yet Fay's desecrating presence now fills a once safe haven; Laurel, hearing the bird brushing against closed doors, herself backs through the door that leads from bedroom to sewing room. This small, cold, dark place seems to allow an even deeper retreat, yet what Laurel discovers there is the self-knowledge she fled: this had been her own room as an infant. Moreover, now it holds all of her mother's "exiled" possessions, all of the keepsakes that organized her memories. As Laurel reads the letters and looks at pictures that open up her mother's stories, "a flood of feeling" finally descends, for her own story is here as well. Reading her name in a letter that her grandmother had written to Becky, Laurel feels grief for all her losses. In the manner of her father, she had turned away from time's thefts, including and especially its destruction of her love for Phil. But in the sewing room, Laurel discovers that "all she had found had found her. The deepest spring in her heart had uncovered itself," as Becky had uncovered her climber, "and it began to flow again" (154). Remembering stories, tales of her parents' and her own connections, brings Laurel back to life.

The sewing room scene, ending part 3 of *The Optimist's Daughter*, sets up the novel's last section, which in one flowing movement takes Laurel through her last morning in a home that must be given over to Fay's inevitable changes. The first passage of part 4 links the overall structure of Laurel's experience to Dorinda's and Janie's. All three characters are aware of the revolving of the seasons, the movement of day into night, and long night struggles into day. Joseph Campbell tells us that for early societies, the Goddess figure was seen as one who "swallows the sun in the west and gives birth to the sun in the east, and it passes through her body at night" (167). In *Barren Ground, Their Eyes Were Watching God,* and *The Optimist's Daughter,* the creating woman character masters time symbolically by her survival of, her connection with, potentially destructive natural processes: night, hurricane, pelting rain, the onset of winter, the beating wings of a trapped bird. Like the other two women's stories, Laurel's contains a climactic scene during which she sees her way out of a trap of despair. As in *Barren Ground,* in *The Optimist's Daughter* a long night's struggle with memory ends in a dawning of new strength. Laurel falls asleep to waken in a house that "was bright and still, like a ship that has tossed all night and come to harbor" (163). Awake, she recognizes that she has dreamed about an actual occurrence which she could recover only in sleep. The image that her dream supplies allows her to leave the past without destroying it, knowing that memory provides adequate compensation against all separations.

Laurel's dream recalls the time that she, with Phil, travelled from Chicago to Mount Salus for her wedding. For the first time, riding the day train, she could see two rivers, the Ohio and the Mississippi, coming together below the bridge at Cairo. Laurel remembers, "They were looking down from a great elevation and all they saw was at the point of coming together, bare trees marching in from the horizon, the rivers moving into one, and as he touched her arm she looked up with him and saw the long, ragged, pencil-faint line of birds within the crystal of the zenith, flying in a V of their own, following the same course down. All they could see was sky, water, birds, light, and confluence" (160). This dream of interconnection, open to her through love, is not fully available to her until she can add memory to the equation. Memory, in the morning after her long vigil with the past, also allows her to see her-

self as she is now, apart from parents, bereft of Phil. She acknowledges
first what Phil taught her as an artist: "He taught her to draw, to work
toward and into her pattern, not to sketch peripheries" (161). Phil was
not an optimist, Laurel remembers, for going within is not an optimist's
strategy. Learning her husband's lesson, Laurel must now work "toward
and into" the patterns of her life, on her own. She must make herself
free from Phil's teaching, as well as her parents'. Confluence, like the
meeting of rivers, tells not about dependence but about a whole new
entity formed from all that has gone before.

From Phil, Laurel received the name "Hand," a name that was hardly
acknowledged in Mount Salus, a stronghold against the incursions of
outsiders and the specter of progress. Significantly, as Laurel prepares
to leave Mount Salus for the last time, she thinks that memory lives not
in possession but in "freed hands, pardoned and freed, and in the heart
that can empty but fill again, in the patterns restored by dreams" (179).
Memory, Laurel learns, can restore the past because it is "vulnerable to
the living moment" (178), not because it is immune to time. As Welty
wrote in "Some Notes on Time in Fiction," "Remembering is so basic and
vital a part of staying alive that it takes on the strength of an instinct of
survival, and acquires the power of an art" (171). Acquiring this power
by her ability to remember "through the blood," as Welty put it in her
essay, Laurel can burn her mother's letters and leave to Fay Phil's bread-
board and her father's house. Her mother's stories go with her on the
journey that will take her back over the confluent course that she and
Phil had watched on their train trip to her parents' home. Laurel knows
that on her plane flight home, the two rivers joining will be "out of sight,
for her, this time, thousands of feet below, but with nothing in between
except thin air" (160). Thus, the confluence that the rivers' joining represents is hers to keep, in the artist's eyes and hands that have at last
been restored by memory to their own appropriate vision.

The Optimist's Daughter ends, like *Barren Ground* and *Their Eyes Were
Watching God,* with a scene designed to show through natural imagery
a self struggling into possession of its own life in nature, in language,
and in time. The achievement of creativity that all three novels celebrate
is announced through voice more than action. Dorinda, Janie, and Laurel make no dramatic gestures and perform no deed that a male mythic

tradition would deem heroic; they do not, in other words, conquer or destroy in order to possess. Yet Dorinda, Janie, and Laurel all achieve heroic stature nonetheless, through language matched to interior vision. The images of traveller, light-bringer, laborer, and seer are brought to bear on each act of voicing. Dorinda, Janie, and Laurel, like their authorial creators, struggle through and in language to shape an articulation of selfhood which allows them to see and to live creatively. There is nothing passive in this celebration of perception: these women, like their creators, will be doers and not just sayers of the word, yet saying-and-seeing the world new becomes the important grounding-point of all significant action. Moreover, the celebration is hardly for women only, but for all who find that their deepest need and satisfaction lie in acts of integration which can show, for any life, the patterns of its connections to self and others. Alice Walker tells us, in one final instance of a woman's quest for roots, direction, and voice, that "Guided by my heritage of a love of beauty and a respect for strength—in search of my mother's garden, I found my own. And perhaps in Africa over two hundred years ago, there was just such a mother; perhaps she painted vivid and daring decorations in oranges and yellows and greens on the walls of her hut; perhaps she sang—in a voice like Roberta Flack's—sweetly over the compounds of her village; perhaps she wove the most stunning mats or told the most ingenious stories of all the village storytellers. Perhaps she was herself a poet—though only her daughter's name is signed to the poems that we know" (*Search* 243). The voice in the garden is finally the artist's voice, a goddess's voice, our mother's voice, our own.

Postscript
Writing Letters Home

When my parents went on trips together, what they took along and how they packed revealed much about them. My father's one small, trim, gray suitcase held only essential items, things that he knew he would need for each day. My mother's larger, canvas plaid case, on the other hand, held whatever she could think of, including medicines for every possible illness, a sweater for unexpected cold snaps, sturdy shoes in case hiking was called for. And after she had packed, she always thought of one more thing, or several, so she would find a grocery bag, or two or three, to carry what was left over. For my mother, never did everything fit neatly into one suitcase. Postscripts, like my mother's extra sacks, are meant for carrying what is left over but still too important to leave out. Postscripts seem, too, a way of ending what one hates to end, of saying that no ending is really final. This postscript carries both intentions.

In *Of Woman Born* (1976, 1986), Adrienne Rich, one of a new generation of women writers with close ties to the South, voices many thoughts that have helped me to see where my explorations were heading. She writes, for instance, of growing up in Baltimore in the segregated 1930s and of having "from birth not only a white, but a Black mother" (253). Thinking of relationships between black and white women, she says, "We have not only been under slavery, lily white wife and dark, sensual concubine; victims of marital violation on the one hand and unpredictable, licensed rape on the other. We have been mothers and daughters

to each other; and although, in the last few years, Black and white feminists have been moving toward a still-difficult sisterhood, there is little
yet known, unearthed, of the time when we were mothers and daughters" (253). Catherine Hammond, a "lily white" plantation wife, could
not, I am sure, imagine such a time. A victim of marital violation herself,
she left her home rather than tolerate her husband's open involvement
with another victim, his black concubine Louisa. Harriet Jacobs voices
the other side of the plantation wife's pain and betrayal in *Incidents in
the Life of a Slave Girl*. She endured the hatred of her master's jealous
wife when James Norcom attempted to force her into sexual relations in
his own home. Nevertheless, after Jacobs fled, she received a mother's
shelter from a white slaveholding woman of Edenton who hid her for
several weeks in her house, at great risk to her own safety. After her
escape to New York, Jacobs found work as a housekeeper, caring for her
white employer's children during a time when she could not make a
home for her own. Even in a southern town dominated by racist ideology, Jacobs found a community of women who were willing, in Jean
Yellin's words, to betray "allegiances of race and class to assert their
stronger allegiance to the sisterhood of all women" (xxxiii). Thus when
Jacobs began writing her autobiography, she could draw upon this support system in projecting her narrative's vision of an alliance uniting
"women of the North" and "two millions of women at the South, still
in bondage" (1). She based the grounds for this vision on the common
experience of motherhood which automatically linked her free white
audience with the sisters she had left in slavery. Throughout her narrative, in scenes that showed slave women separated from their children,
she stressed the hopes that every mother cherished for her daughters.
The words that came to her as she assessed her infant daughter's future
—"Slavery is terrible for men; but it is far more terrible for women"—
defined a struggle that belonged to all women in a patriarchal society.
They also provide a bridge joining her to Catherine Hammond in this
plantation wife's firm conviction that slavery "is dead and I for one don't
want it back."

Rich challenges women to create bonds of motherhood, daughterhood, and sisterhood not limited by restraints of race and class. Her
poem, "Education of a Novelist" (in *Your Native Land, Your Life* 1986),

draws upon Ellen Glasgow's description of her relationship with her black nurse, Lizzie Jones. Rich emphasizes Lizzie Jones's nurturing role and Glasgow's promise, never kept, that she would teach her "Mammy" how to read. Using Glasgow's own words from *The Woman Within* to stress the hopes and betrayals inherent in black/white relationships, Rich admits, "It's not enough using your words to damn you, Ellen: they could have been my own: this criss-cross map of kept and broken promises" (40). Rich's sense of how tentatively black and white women reach out to one another finds expression in Jacobs's *Incidents in the Life of a Slave Girl,* but also in the novels we have explored by Glasgow, Hurston, and Welty. In *Barren Ground,* Dorinda's most satisfactory companion was Fluvanna, a black woman who came to live with her after both her parents died. Glasgow, perhaps envisioning the relationship that she and Lizzie Jones might have enjoyed, writes: "The affection between the two women had outgrown the slender tie of mistress and maid, and had become as strong and elastic as the bond that holds relatives together" (340). Although Dorinda still retained "an inherited feeling of condescension," the two "trusted each other without discretion and without restraint." Zora Neale Hurston, too, saw that white and black women might sustain each other in a natural alliance. In *Their Eyes Were Watching God,* Janie's voice during her trial connected her to a group of white women who listened to her, as neither the black or the white men did, and who rallied to protect her. And in *The Optimist's Daughter,* Laurel in her grief found her greatest comfort in the arms of her father's housekeeper, Missouri, who told her, "All birds got to fly" (168). Missouri, alone, of all Laurel's Mount Salus women friends, ratified her choice to leave her parents' world. The ties in these novels are not boldly dramatized, yet they are "strong and elastic" nonetheless, breaking what Rich calls "the double silence of sexism and racism" that culturally interferes with relationships between black and white women.

In *Of Woman Born,* Rich writes poignantly of another deeply personal relationship, the bonds of mothers and their daughters. She draws on her memories of her mother, who was born in a southern town, "a young belle, who could have married at any time," but who also "trained seriously for years both as a concert pianist and a composer" (221). In her marriage, Rich's mother gave up her plans for a career: "my father, brilliant, ambitious, possessed by his own drive, assumed that she would give her life over to the enhancement of his" (221). The tension between Rich's parents and her anger at feeling that her mother "had chosen my father over me" (222) echo in many ways the experiences that Ellen Glasgow, Zora Neale Hurston, and Eudora Welty remember in their auto-biographies. "A part of me," Rich confesses, "identifies too much with her" (223–24). Her recognition fills in one of the silences of the earlier women's autobiographies, for she says, "There was, is, in most of us, a girl-child still longing for a woman's nurture, tenderness, and approval, a woman's power exerted in our defense, a woman's smell and touch and voice, a woman's strong arms around us in moments of fear and pain" (224). That cry, she says, "is the germ of our desire to create a world in which strong mothers and strong daughters will be a matter of course" (225). Glasgow, Hurston, and Welty were able in their autobi-ographies to voice the girl-child's longing for the strong mother, yet all three voiced even more strongly their need to take a different direction from the one that their mothers did not really choose but nonetheless endured.

Glasgow, Hurston, and Welty all became strong daughters and in their novels created characters who were strong daughters. Yet these authors never became mothers, nor does Dorinda in *Barren Ground,* Janie in *Their Eyes Were Watching God,* or Laurel in *The Optimist's Daughter.* Perhaps Glasgow's Dorinda gives the most honest reason when she says to her-self, "Mother love was a wonderful thing, . . . a wonderful and a ruinous thing!" (315). In this comment Glasgow expresses Dorinda's exaspera-tion with her mother's self-sacrifice, an exasperation that the author perhaps shared, from her experience with her own martyred mother. In Glasgow, Hurston, and Welty's generation, motherhood could be heroic, a risk of self in giving life to unknown others. Yet motherhood's demands were made to seem incompatible with other kinds of creating, with other ways of reaching out to and gaining power over the unknown, especially the unknown in oneself. It is quite possible that these three writers felt the ambivalence that Rich exposes when she suggests that "into the mere notion of 'mothering' we may carry, as daughters, negative echoes of our own mothers' martyrdom, the burden of their valiant, necessarily lim-ited efforts on our behalf, the confusion of their double messages" (253).

In turning away from mothers and from motherhood, perhaps Glasgow, Hurston, Welty, and their characters were turning away from their own vulnerability, their fear of powerlessness.

The denial of the mother, Rich writes, "represents a timidity of the imagination"; women cannot realistically opt to be daughters, or "free spirits," rather than "mothers," who are "defined as eternal givers." For, as she urges, "We are, none of us, 'either' mothers or daughters; to our amazement, confusion, and greater complexity, we are both" (253). This recognition constitutes an imperative for women seeking empowering connections because, as she notes, "any radical vision of sisterhood de-mands that we reintegrate" the mother and daughter in ourselves. Rich returns us, through her vision, to the idea of Demeter and Persephone—to the quest for wholeness that this ancient matriarchal story celebrates. Two southern women's novels of the 1980s seem to me to answer Rich's call for reintegration of mother and daughter, Demeter and Persephone. Alice Walker in *The Color Purple* and Lee Smith in *Fair and Tender Ladies* create women who, alienated within themselves and searching for connections, achieve reintegrations which restore their worlds, inner and outer, to wholeness. The southern women writers of this study, through both autobiographical and fictional quests, have provided chal-lenging versions of Demeter's separation from and search for self; *The Color Purple* and *Fair and Tender Ladies* have their roots in these earlier stories. Yet Walker and Smith add a new dimension, the discovery of sisterhood, to their women characters' quests. Through stories of sisters, lost but reunited in language, their novels enlarge the possibilities for woman's connections to others and herself.

Alice Walker and Lee Smith, black woman and white woman, are daughters, mothers, novelists, and southerners. In *The Color Purple* (1982) and *Fair and Tender Ladies* (1988), they create characters who are mothers, sisters, daughters, and writers. Celie and Nettie in *The Color Purple* and Ivy Rowe in *Fair and Tender Ladies* write the most intimate and private of texts, letters. In both works, the letters that mean the most are ones that they address to sisters long lost. Celie and Nettie represent two alternatives for black girls in the South. Nettie runs away from a southern community in which black women were indeed stig-matized as the mules of the world. Celie opts to endure her lot in this community, wordlessly accepting the brutality that men inflict simply because she sees no other way to survive. Through the many years that the sisters write to one another, they receive no answers, and for at least part of the time, Celie believes that Nettie is dead. Both survive by keeping the absent sister alive in letters. As Nettie tells Celie, "when I don't write to you I feel as bad as I do when I don't pray, locked up in myself and choking on my own heart" (122). Ivy Rowe, in *Fair and Tender Ladies,* writes to her sister Silvaney for much the same purpose. Silvaney, sent away from her family to a home for the mentally ill, could not read or understand Ivy's letters. Yet even when Ivy finds out after many years that Silvaney died during a flu epidemic, she continues to write to the sister who had never been able to respond. In one of her earlier letters, she says, "Oh Silvaney! sometimes I think I made you up to suit me!" (107). Writing to absent sisters becomes a means of escape, a means of making connections, and thus, a means of transformation.

Celie and Ivy are in spirit poets, artists, and creators, yet for much of their lives only their letters give them a vehicle to express these identities. Poverty, racism, and sexism decree that their lives will be spent serving men, bearing children, keeping house, feeding, cleaning, planting, and dying. Both women very early lose their chance to be daughters —nurtured, protected young girls who have the option to grow and to explore. While still in their early teens, they bear children, becoming mothers and givers who never have the opportunity freely to decide the destinies of their own bodies. In accepting and nurturing children, Celie and Ivy Rowe gain a dimension that Glasgow's Dorinda, Hurston's Janie, and Welty's Laurel lack. The costs of mothering are high, yet Celie and Ivy struggle to connect children and home to other patterns of creativity. The reward is one which Alice Walker noted in an essay about her daughter: "We are together, my child and I. Mother and child, yes, but *sisters* really, against whatever denies us all that we are" (*Search* 382).

Celie's struggle against forces denying both her and her children their right to identity begins when, at age fourteen, she is raped repeatedly by the man she believes is her father. This man, actually her stepfather, gives away the two children that Celie bears as a result of his rapes. After he marries again, he sends Celie away too, to be the wife of a widower with four children. Albert wants her as a slave, someone to keep house, care for the children, and gratify his sexual needs.[1] He beats her, he tells his son, because she is his wife and because beatings and sex are "all women good for" (30). Celie's response is, in a way, creative: "I make myself wood. I say to myself, Celie, you a tree" (30). Denied the right to have anything of her own, even her own children, Celie becomes a wooden "Everymother," always giving, losing herself in meeting the demands of others. Contrasted to Celie is Shug Avery, her husband's lover and a nightclub singer. Shug represents a very different idea of woman, a sexually alluring free spirit who has abandoned her children in order to escape the communal definitions of woman that are responsible for Celie's victimization. Shug is "womanly," yet acts "manly" in that she can "speak her mind and the devil take the hindmost," qualities that Albert, at least, associates with men (236). Through Shug, Celie becomes "womanly" in this "manly" way as well. With Shug as teacher, Celie realizes that she is more than every man's sexual object, more than any child's mother: she is creative in self-designing ways—a quilt maker, later a designer of pants, and one who has been, all her life, a writer, a maker of the most personal kind of text.

Celie's letters, at first stumbling and hardly coherent, reflect in their progression her growth into voice and selfhood. At first Celie writes her letters to God. Alphonso, her stepfather, warned her to "not never tell nobody but God" (11) about his sexual attacks. Obediently, she accepts this male restriction of her voice, yet in her shame she writes to God instead of talking to Him. In writing letters, she discovers a uniquely personal form of self-expression. The God to whom she writes may be, indeed, only "a man," as she later evaluates Him, "just like all the other mens I know. Trifling, forgitful and lowdown" (175). Yet as a listener whom she creates out of her own need, God keeps her alive in giving her ideas and feelings a shape and a place to go. As she tells her sister, "Long as I can spell G-o-d I got somebody along" (26). In writing her letters, Celie creates and in creating, survives. Albert, in keeping her sister Nettie's letters from her, threatens that survival. He, in effect, robs her of herself as well as of her sister. This theft is of a piece with his beatings and his constant belittling of her. When, after many years, Shug discovers that Albert has intercepted all of Nettie's letters, she helps Celie to recover them. With her sister's words in her possession, Celie recovers her voice and her self as well. Celie's first act of speaking in her own voice occurs when she changes the audience for her letters, addressing them no longer to an abstract male God but to the sister who, as correspondent, validates her own existence. Nettie's letters to her bring knowledge of her children, of her culture's roots in Africa, and thus of a self completely different from the image of silent giver to which she has conformed in her life with Alphonso and Albert.

Celie's second act of voicing occurs when she turns on Albert in her story's most dramatic scene, one reminiscent of Janie Crawford's attack on Joe Starks in *Their Eyes Were Watching God.* With her large extended family gathered around the dinner table to witness, Celie says to Albert, "You a lowdown dog. . . . It's time to leave you and enter into the Creation. And your dead body just the welcome mat I need" (181). Once they recover from the shock of hearing Celie's voice, the other women speak up as well, forming an accusing, liberating chorus. Celie finds that she has self-made weapons, her sister and children, to use against Albert. "Nettie and my children coming home soon," she says, "and when she do, all us together gon whup your ass." The concept of sisterhood— women as protectors, as listeners, as sharers, as cocreators in language —becomes a tangible force through the letters in which Celie frees her voice.

Ivy Rowe, of *Fair and Tender Ladies,* resembles Celie in that she must fight all her life against the fate that her society prescribes for women. A young girl growing up in the Virginia mountains, Ivy cannot see how her future looks back at her in the assessment that she gives of her mother's situation: "My momma was young and so pretty when she come riding up Sugar Fork, but she does not look pretty now, she looks awful, like her face is hanted, she has had too much on her" (15).[2] Her mother's "too much" includes a life of unrelenting poverty on a mountain farm, a dying husband, nine children, and the endless round of "chores," as Ivy calls them—planting, milking, cooking, cleaning, nursing. Ivy plans to be a writer, to create poems about love, to be in love, but not, she adds, "to have a lot of babys thogh" (15). Very early she understands that babies gave her mother's face its "hanted" look, yet she fails to understand that the "love" she craves will only lead her, like her mother, to the fate she tries to escape through romantic fantasies. After her father's death, when Ivy moves with her mother to a town away from her holler, a different escape route seems to open up through opportunities for schooling. Miss Torrington, a Boston teacher, responds to Ivy's craving for knowledge and offers to take her north to be educated as a lady. Ivy turns between choices that indicate her inner dividedness: will she be a writer of romances, a pristine, "old maid" teacher, or an indomitable mountain woman like her grandmother, who lives by the folk wisdom of her beloved hills?

Given the realities of her time, place, and situation, however, Ivy has no choices. The dream of going to Boston dies when she becomes pregnant, "ruint," as she puts it, since she will not marry her child's father. Ivy describes her thoughts when she discovers that she is going to have a baby: "At first I could not immagine the baby inside and then I could. . . . And then, I cannot explain it Silvaney, I *was* that little baby caught inside of my own self and dying to escape. But I could not. I could not ever get out, I was caught for ever and ever inside myself" (122). Ivy's woman's body, her world of poverty and ignorance, her dreams of a perfect romantic love all combine to make a prison in which daughter must become mother, trapped in the child whom she has created, her self held by what her womb holds.

Unlike Celie, Ivy has the compensation, in motherhood, of beholding through her child some of her own creative spirit. When her first daughter, Joli, is born, she writes to a woman who had condescended to feel sorry for her: "Do not even bother to dislike me, nor pity me, nor anything else. . . . My little baby Joli Rowe was born September 10, 1918. She is all mine, I have never had a thing of my own before" (141). Yet the trap which Ivy envisioned during her first pregnancy closes in more tightly with the birth of each new baby. Married to Oakley Fox, Ivy has four more children after Joli. To Miss Torrington she writes simply, "To answer your question, I do not read much any more" (192). But writing to Silvaney, after her fourth baby, Maudy, is born, Ivy can say, "It is like I was a girl for such a long time, years and years, and then all of a sudden I have got to be an old woman, with no in between. . . . I never get out and go places any more, Silvaney. A woman just can't go off and leave so many children" (195). Defined as mother, Ivy feels that she must bury other possibilities for herself. When she does escape, running away for a brief time with a man named aptly "Honey Breeding," a sense of the enormity of her duties as mother strikes with cruel force: her daughter LuIda died while she was gone. Only writing gives Ivy an escape from the life that her husband defines when he tells her, "Get up, Ivy, and take care of your children" (240).

Silvaney functions for Ivy in much the same way that, in *The Color Purple,* Nettie functions for Celie. Each writer, in connecting herself to a lost sister through letters, creates a larger identity for herself than the roles of wife and childbearer allow. Ivy's first letter in *Fair and Tender Ladies* is addressed to a "Pen Friend" in Holland. To the faraway "Hanneke," Ivy the mountain child pours out stories that give her narrowly bounded life rich possibilities. Yet the letter is never sent; her teacher says that it is "too long and not appropriate" (20). Ivy prepares a second draft, announcing to Hanneke that "I want to be a famous writter when I grow up" (21). Although Hanneke of Holland never replies, Ivy continues to write letters to her, as well as to several other family members and to her teacher. Yet only when Silvaney, her wild, half-crazy sister, is taken away to an institution, does Ivy finds the pen friend she needs. Silvaney represents the self that Ivy buries in order to fit into the patterns of woman's work in her home on Sugar Fork: "we are the same sometimes it is like we are one" (17), she explains. Silvaney and Ivy both suffer as they watch their mother's desperation, their father's slow death, the violent passions that seem to sweep continually over family members. Silvaney responds by running wildly, silently, through the hills; Ivy responds with words, in long, wild letters combining mountain legends with her own fantasies and experiences. In her letters, Ivy makes order out of the chaos that drives Silvaney deeper into wordless madness.

The tendency that Ivy and Silvaney share most deeply is their love of stories. In one scene that is symbolic of Ivy's inner life, she describes two elderly sisters, who live completely isolated far up on "Hell Mountain" without any means of support except for food that people bring them to hear their stories. "I think myself they live on storys" (33), Ivy says. When they visit her family's cabin in the dead of winter, they spend the night telling mountain tales, bringing rare laughter to the desolate cabin. These mysterious mountain women, telling their sustaining stories back and forth in one blended voice, are doubles of Ivy-Silvaney, the con-

struct of sisterhood that Ivy creates to give her writing direction and
meaning. Years later, when family members find all the letters that Ivy
wrote to Silvaney, Ivy explains that while she had known of Silvaney's
death, years before, "it didn't *matter*. Silvaney, you see, was a part of me,
my other side, my other half, my heart" (312). As for the letters, they
"didn't mean anything. Not to the dead girl Silvaney, of course—*nor to
me*. Nor had they ever. It was the *writing* of them, that signified" (313).
Silvaney exists forcefully for Ivy as the part of herself who listens but
has no voice, who lives on stories but has none of her own. In writing
to Silvaney, Ivy connects voice and listener, teller and tale; in making
these connections, she creates a sustaining, integrated image of herself.

Both *The Color Purple* and *Fair and Tender Ladies* end with reunions
that restore creating women to each other and themselves. Celie inherits
her mother's house, which becomes a model of her identity—mother,
daughter, and artist. She decorates the house in colors of women's spirit
—pink for Shug, red, yellow, and of course, purple for herself. When
Shug arrives, she acknowledges Celie's new role as matriarch when she
says, "I missed you more than I missed my own mama" (248). The house
prepared for reunion is finally filled when Nettie returns from Africa,
where she lived, along with Celie's children and a missionary family,
for most of the years that she and Celie had been separated. Nettie
brings home her missionary husband and Celie's children, including a
new African daughter, the young woman whom Celie's son has married.
Celie's world is rejuvenated in her version of Demeter's story, a story
of reunion with a sister who completes the design of her life. "I think
this the youngest us ever felt," Celie writes in her last letter to God. The
God of her earlier letters, a man "big and old and tall and graybearded
and white," disappears just as the patriarch disappears in the Eleusinian
rituals belonging to Demeter.[3] In his place, Celie finds and addresses
"Dear God. Dear stars, dear trees, dear sky, dear peoples. Dear Everything"—in other words, an image of the power that resides in herself, a
reintegrated woman, at home in the world.

In *Fair and Tender Ladies,* too, Ivy comes into possession of her
mother's house, high in the mountains where she feels most at home.
After her husband Oakley's death, Ivy writes to Silvaney: "not one hour
for the rest of my life will go by without me missing Oakley and that's

a fact. But I will tell you another fact which is just as true, it hit me yesterday. . . . I can make up my own life now whichever way I want to, it is like I am a girl again, for I am not beholden to a soul" (277). Ivy makes her home a refuge for children—her own, her friends', even her children's children. "Send him on," she tells Joli, who has asked if Ivy will keep her son, David, for a time; "it will keep me young," she explains (277). In her last letter to Joli, Ivy asserts her right, although she is old and ill, to stay in her cabin, up among the mountains which now look "different, strange and new" (313). Ivy's mountains, like her life, never stay the same; change, in cycles of death and renewal, is the story, a Demeter story, that she reads from them and associates with her own spirit. Ivy's final letter is to Silvaney, her "other half," telling of a March snow, which "brings good luck, and a pretty spring" (313). In a kind of dream that she reports to Silvaney, memories of her family merge in her mind with the childhood poems and stories that she loved. "I never became a writer atall" (315), she says, yet this letter, like all her letters, tells a different story. She says at the start of it, "I am dying to write I am dying to" (313), and so, close to death, she continues her life-long, urgent effort of setting down her world in words. The final sound that Ivy's letter records is "the old bell ringing like I rang it to call them home." Her letters call home the family that she recreates in writing to her sister, herself.

We began this story with Catherine Hammond, the plantation wife who came into possession of her home when the Civil War destroyed the patriarchal foundations of her husband's ruthless dominion. We read her letter, and also one that the former slave Harriet Jacobs wrote when she, too, was able after the Civil War to return home. Jacobs wrote to Ednah Dow Cheney while sitting in her grandmother's house in Edenton, North Carolina, remembering how that home had been, even in slavery times, a place of women's power and protection. In a later fictional homecoming, Ellen Glasgow's Dorinda found her life in restoring the farm that was her mother's inheritance. Through the land's changes she recognized her own capacities for change. The home which was once barren ground became a place where Dorinda could celebrate, in symbolic autumns, harvests of personal growth. Following a pattern not unlike Dorinda's, Zora Neale Hurston's Janie returned to the home she inherited from a husband who tried unsuccessfully to keep her from having a life, or a story, of her own to tell. Sitting on the porch of her house, she celebrated her narrative of self-discovery with her friend Pheoby, who paid tribute to the transforming powers of Janie's gift of story by saying, "You look like youse yo' own daughter" (14). And in one last version of Demeter's legend, Eudora Welty's Laurel McKelva leaves the home that her father surrendered to time and the future when he married Fay. In returning to Chicago at the end of her story, she returns to her own life in time. In Chicago she had left behind a project, designing a theatre curtain; now that curtain will rise on the life she had never before felt free to live. Back in Mount Salus, her mother's roses will bloom, and, in memory, Laurel will keep what she found in her mother's writing desk, letters that Becky McKelva had stored "according to their time and place" (135). In their writing—letters, autobiographies, novels —these women found voices with which to tell stories celebrating home, creativity, and connections. Their voices establish visions of sisterhood, patterns of women's reintegration of mother, daughter, and self.

In a postscript to *Fair and Tender Ladies,* Lee Smith pays tribute to her friend, the Appalachian poet Kathryn Stripling Byer, and acknowledges her novel's assimilation of the "legends, history, songs, and tales" of her home country in the southwest Virginia mountains. The book's title comes from one of Byer's poems, "Weep-Willow," which tells of a mountain woman storyteller, a balladeer who calls to "fair and tender ladies" and sings knowingly of "woman's darkest hours." The poem and the novel take their inspiration from the women who make their lives on these lonesome, haunting mountains, women often inarticulate in themselves but sources for a woman artist's sustaining songs. Likewise, Alice Walker's book *In Search of Our Mothers' Gardens* pays tribute to black women who, within their culture, found few outlets for their creativity but who opened the way for the songs, the poems, the novels of daughters to come. In particular Walker acknowledges her own mother's role in making her characters' voices when she says, "So many of the stories that I write, that we all write, are my mother's stories. . . . I have absorbed not only the stories themselves, but something of the manner in which she spoke, something of the urgency that involves the knowledge that her stories—like her life—must be recorded" (240). Adrienne

Rich writes that "the quality of the mother's life—however embattled and unprotected—is her primary bequest to her daughter" (247). We have listened here to the voices of black women and white women who wrote to separate themselves from patriarchal creeds promoting woman's weakness and to connect themselves to ancient mothers' wisdom affirming woman's creative power. From these women writing—some anonymously, some with pseudonyms, some in slavery, all at risk—we have received a bequest that will honor them and us for as long as we can read their letters on the page, the bequest of woman's voice in southern story.

NOTES

Works cited frequently are identified throughout the text by the following ab-
breviations:

BG	Glasgow, *Barren Ground*
CM	Glasgow, *A Certain Measure*
MM	Hurston, *Mules and Men*
OWB	Welty, *One Writer's Beginnings*
Search	Walker, *In Search of Our Mothers' Gardens*
"Versions"	Olney, "Some Versions of Memory"
Women's Ways	Belenky et al., *Women's Ways of Knowing*
WW	Glasgow, *The Woman Within*

Introduction: Southern Daughters of Time

1. Mary Field Belenky et al., *Women's Ways of Knowing*, 18. The authors use
the term "voice" because, as they explain, they discovered in their interviews
with women that "'voice' was more than an academic shorthand for a person's
point of view. Well after we were into our interviews with women, we became
aware that it is a metaphor that can apply to many aspects of women's experience and development. In describing their lives, women commonly talked about
voice and silence: 'speaking up,' 'speaking out,' 'being silenced,' 'not being heard,'
'really listening,' 'really talking,' 'words as weapons,' 'feeling deaf and dumb,'
'having no words,' 'saying what you mean,' 'listening to be heard,' and so on in
an endless variety of connotations all having to do with sense of mind, self-
worth, and feelings of isolation from or connections to others." These are the
connotations that I have in mind in using the word "voice" in this study.

2. Barbara Welter provides an analysis of this cultural ideal in her article,
"The Cult of True Womanhood: 1820–1860." She says, "The attributes of True
Womanhood, by which a woman judged herself and was judged by her husband,
her neighbors and society could be divided into four cardinal virtues—piety,
purity, submissiveness and domesticity. Put them all together and they spelled
mother, daughter, sister, wife—woman" (152). She quotes Emerson's opinion
that woman is "more vulnerable, more infirm, more mortal than man" (162).

3. Anne Goodwyn Jones in *Tomorrow Is Another Day* and Louise Westling in *Sacred Groves and Ravaged Gardens* deal extensively with problems that women writers have faced as a result of growing up within the South's patriarchal structure. Jones, studying women writers from 1859 through 1936, begins with the assumption that "the idea of southern womanhood specifically denies the self" and notes that the concept of the southern lady, while it has "much in common with the ideas of the British Victorian lady and of American true womanhood," has had an even stronger influence, primarily because "the identity of the South is contingent in part upon the persistence of its tradition of the lady" (4). Louise Westling, in her study of Eudora Welty, Flannery O'Connor, and Carson McCullers, discusses how these women benefited from a strong, distinctive tradition of women's writing in the South. Her study traces ways in which all three of these writers "were permanently marked by their upbringing as Southern girls" (54). Both Jones and Westling stress that the South's veneration of the lady determined the southern woman writer's definition of feminine identity. Both books provide valuable, thorough introductions to the cultural forces that shaped the white southern woman writer's sense of herself.

4. The "daughter's sensibility" is a concept that Barbara Mossberg defines in her study, *Emily Dickinson: When a Writer Is a Daughter*. Mossberg finds that Dickinson's identity as daughter "shapes her poetic stance": "Whether Dickinson exhibits a dutiful sensibility—timid, self-sacrificing, anxious, eager to please, seeking parental approval, dependent, and vulnerable—or a rebellious sensibility—jaunty, angry, scornful, ironic, convinced of her own uniqueness, power, autonomy, and superiority—she is a daughter trying to commune with and break away from a patriarchy that eclipses women" (11). The women of my study identify, as writers, with the "daughter's sensibility" for the same purpose as Dickinson: they want both to "commune with" as well as to "break away from" southern patriarchy.

5. Simpson defines the "southern aesthetic of memory" as in part a "quest to transform history through memory into art" (216). He refers to Eudora Welty's essay, "Some Notes on Time in Fiction," in showing how the modern southern storyteller "has been shaped . . . by the exigent force of the memory against history" (215). History, which he defines as "an ineluctable process or series of processes, which may be regarded either as teleological or blankly purposeless" (215), can be transfigured through memory. Glasgow, Hurston, and Welty valorize memory in the manner that Simpson outlines, as "an instinct of survival against history"; for these writers, remembering is, to use Simpson's words, "an art of the psychic—the spiritual—survival of the individual" threatened with

isolation and dehumanization as creatures of history. Women writers, as we shall see, have gender-related reasons for turning to memory as a way to gain power over the historical exigencies of their lives.

6. In her collection of "womanist" prose, *In Search of Our Mothers' Gardens,* Walker contrasts her daughter, who is a source of support and comfort, to those outsiders who have "purged my face from history and herstory and left mystory just that, a mystery" (382).

CHAPTER ONE
Naming the Father:
The Stories of Catherine Hammond and Harriet Jacobs

1. Bertram Wyatt-Brown, 120. Wyatt-Brown notes how in the South, "distinguished surnames" often replaced ordinary Christian "first" names, a practice by which, perhaps, "the threat of family dissolution could be prevented" (120). He adds that when surnames were taken from the maternal side, it "did not necessarily represent veneration of the mother, but rather honored her father."

2. William Byrd to the Earl of Orrery, July 5, 1726, quoted in Willie Lee Rose, *Slavery and Freedom.* Rose's essay, "The Domestication of Domestic Slavery," traces the evolution of the ideal of the patriarch through generations of southern slaveholders. Rose says that while the plantation master self-consciously promoted his estate as a patriarchy, a "domestic hierarchy" in which he had "star billing," his own blood family "was actually more of a matriarchy, because of the paramount role of his wife in child-rearing, in household management, and in religious and social matters" (29).

3. Jean Fagin Yellin, in her invaluable introduction to the Harvard edition (1987) of *Incidents,* traces Jacobs's self-construction of her narrative through letters that she wrote during the 1850s. She concludes that "both its style and its content . . . are completely consistent with Jacobs's private correspondence and with her pseudonymous public letters to the newspapers—which unquestionably she wrote by herself" (xxi).

4. James Henry Hammond's story is told in Drew Faust's *James Henry Hammond and the Old South: A Design for Mastery.* Catherine Hammond appears as a shadowy figure in this account. Faust says that Catherine "meekly accepted" Hammond's views of "her own incapacity" (313), an assessment that her letters to Marcus Hammond, discussed here, challenge.

5. Jean Fagin Yellin has uncovered information about James Norcom, Harriet Jacobs's "Dr. Flint," from family papers housed at the North Carolina State Ar-

chives and legal documents such as wills and county tax lists. Ironically, were it not for the fame of his runaway slave, James Norcom would have passed into oblivion.

6. Faust gives extensive treatment to this episode in her biography. Hammond "acknowledged that he might have sired children by both Louisa and her mother" (315). He steadfastly refused to sell them. At one point he agreed to send Louisa to Charleston to be a maidservant to the Fitzsimons family. But Faust notes that even after Catherine returned and set up housekeeping with her husband at their new estate, Redcliffe, "Sally and Louisa Johnson remained on the plantation too, though in field quarters far away from the main house" (317).

7. Catherine Hammond, like most southern gentlewomen, found comfort in her religion, in seeing God's hand at work in her affairs. Ellen Glasgow comments on the role that religion played in reconciling women to their lot: "I think it is almost impossible to over-estimate the part that religion, in one form or another, has played in the lives of southern women. Nothing else could have made them accept with meekness the wing of the chicken and the double standard of morals" (quoted in Linda Wagner, *Ellen Glasgow: Beyond Convention* 4).

8. James Olney, in "'I Was Born': Slave Narratives, Their Status as Autobiography and as Literature," discusses slave narrative conventions, remarking that they were so "firmly established . . . that one can imagine a sort of master outline drawn from the great narratives and guiding the lesser ones." He includes in his "master outline" the requirement of a preface, in which "the reader is told that the narrative is a 'plain, unvarnished tale,'" and "a first sentence beginning, 'I was born'" (152–53). William Andrews, in his book-length study of slave narratives, *To Tell a Free Story*, recounts that Jacobs's *Incidents in the Life of a Slave Girl* was considered inauthentic because it employed narrative techniques that we associate with novels—in particular, "reconstructed dialogue"—instead of adhering to a standard, straightforward recitation of a representative "life" in slavery (270–71).

9. Jacobs, 114. Yellin notes that Jacobs was "not the first Afro-American to use Cowper's phrase. In 1838 the phrase 'From the loop-holes of Retreat' appeared as an epigraph to 'The Curtain,' a column in *Freedom's Journal*" (Jacobs 277, n. 1).

CHAPTER TWO
Prodigal Daughters:
The Journeys of Ellen Glasgow, Zora Neale Hurston, and Eudora Welty

1. Hurston's date of birth, as Robert Hemenway has documented, raises many questions. While she herself cited several dates, ranging from 1898 to 1910,

census records establish that she was born on January 7, 1891 (Hemenway x–xi). When Alice Walker ordered a headstone for Hurston's grave in Fort Pierce, Florida, the dates that she listed were 1901–1960 (*Search* 107).

2. Estelle Jelinek, distinguishing between men's and women's autobiographies, theorizes that "Irregularity rather than orderliness informs the self-portraits by women. The narratives of their lives are often not chronological and progressive but disconnected, fragmentary, or organized into self-sustained units rather than connecting chapters" (17). The three women autobiographers of my study tend to write in the nonchronological, disjunctive mode that Jelinek sees as a dominant trait of women's autobiographies as a class. Robert Hemenway's complaint that in *Dust Tracks* Hurston "never really explains the inner workings" of her "metamorphosis" from "mischievous child" into "famous black novelist and anthropologist" (xxxviii) is answered in large part by Jelinek's theory. And *One Writer's Beginnings,* according to Peggy Whitman Prenshaw, "closely conforms to the patterns of women's autobiographies identified by Estelle C. Jelinek" (230).

3. J. R. Raper, in *Without Shelter,* provides some documentation of the rumor and notes that it "gains added support" from the fact that Ellen Glasgow made relationships between southern gentlemen and black concubines "a recurring theme in [her] more important novels" (29).

4. What Hurston calls her "word-changing" is a form of "specifying." This feature of black oral culture can be defined as the practice of "name calling," which, according to Susan Willis, "insists on a direct relationship between the names and the person being named," with the name-caller guaranteeing the relationship (16). As Willis notes, specifying is a "self-affirming form of discourse" (31). When Hurston shows herself in the act of specifying with her father as her target, she claims a form of strength that would be respected specifically within the rural southern community that she wants, as author, both to re-enter and to transform.

5. Welty, in her essay "Some Notes on Time in Fiction," distinguishes between fictional time and clock time, saying that "Fictional time may be more congenial to us than clock time, precisely for human reasons" (168). In *One Writer's Beginnings,* Welty associates her father with the clock time which, in her essay, she interprets as having an "arbitrary, bullying power." Autobiographically, Welty associates herself with fictional time, which can, according to the contrast she develops in her essay, control clock time. Fiction, she says in the essay, "penetrates chronological time to reach our deeper version of time that's given to us by the way we think and feel." One of the triumphs that her autobiography records is her acceptance of memory as her means of reaching, in her

fiction, a "version of time" that goes far deeper than the version she associates with her father.

CHAPTER THREE
The Voice in the Garden:
Creating Women in the Modern Southern Novel

1. The characters of these novels all marry, changing their maiden names; Janie, with three husbands, has a string of possibilities for her last name—she is, in effect, Janie Crawford Killicks Starks Woods. In retaining these women's maiden names for this study, I want to emphasize the identity of daughter that takes precedence, in the novels, over the identity of wife. All three women are widowed; their full discovery of self takes place when, as widows, they go far back in memory and retrace their lives from the time that their identities were fixed within their families. Thus it seems in one sense "proper" to call them by their patronymic. Gilbert and Gubar offer useful insights on how a woman should be "called": "For women of our culture, however, a proper name is at best problematic; even as it 'inscribes' her into the present discourse of society by designating her role as her father's daughter, her patronymic effaces her matrilineage and thus erases her own position in the discourse of the future. Her 'proper' name, therefore, is always in a way *im*proper because it is not, in the French sense, *propre,* her own, either to have or to give" (237).

2. In each of these three novels, the author translates memories of highly charged personal experiences into art. Glasgow wrote that *Barren Ground* was a book "which I had gathered up, as a rich harvest, from the whole of my life" (*WW* 270). Alice Walker tells us concerning Hurston that "everything she experienced in Eatonville she eventually put into her books. Indeed, one gets the feeling that she tried over and over again with the same material until she felt she had gotten it right. She got it perfectly right in *Their Eyes Were Watching God,* in 1937" (*I Love Myself* 176). And in her study of Welty's revisions of *The Optimist's Daughter,* which appeared first as a story in the *New Yorker* (1969), Helen Hurt Tiegreen quotes Welty as saying (in the introduction to the Franklin Mint edition of the novel, 1980) that "Though the story was not 'like' my own, it was *intimate* with my own—a closer affinity. Writing it involved my deepest feelings, their translation into the events of the story was demanding of my ability as no other novel, so far, has been" (200).

3. Linda W. Wagner points out that "Dorinda is, in a sense, regaining her family's reputation as well; the land had been in her mother's family and her

father had been able to do little but lose what soil had been tillable. Reclaiming the land is a responsibility of the matriarchal line, in one sense" (74).

4. Elizabeth A. Meese associates Janie's idea of experience as the prerequisite for knowledge with both black tribal tradition and Jacques Derrida's point that "the logocentrist or logocentric impulse is rocked by historical events, rocked by things that happen." Janie's assertion, "you got to *go* there to *know* there," indicates how she has found internally the means of liberating/transforming herself and, in consequence, her story. As Meese says, "Having gone there, you are changed, and the story you have to tell is a different story" (51).

5. Alan Dundes, in his book *Mother Wit from the Laughing Barrel,* provides three connotations for "mother wit" that we can apply to Janie's language: it is, first, "a popular term in black speech referring to common sense"; secondly, it is "the kind of good sense not necessarily learned from books or in school"; and thirdly, "with its connotation of collective wisdom acquired by the experience of living and from generations past," it is "often expressed in folklore" (xiv).

6. This assessment of *Their Eyes Were Watching God* as a young black woman's Portrait of the Artist has been made both by Meese (52) and by Trudy Bloser Bush (1035).

7. Louise Westling discusses in detail the Demeter theme as it operates in Welty's first novel, *Delta Wedding* (1946). Westling says that "almost by instinct [Welty] fixed upon ancient symbolic patterns which once were central to a world dominated by maternal powers in an idealized garden setting" (78).

Postscript: Writing Letters Home

1. Calvin C. Hernton asserts that *The Color Purple* is a slave narrative, "in both form and content." Its subject matter "is the substance out of which all slave narratives are made—Oppression and the Process of Liberation" (3). Read in this light, Celie takes us back to Harriet Jacobs; Hernton writes that Alice Walker "repossessed the genre, for it belongs as much to women as to men, and she *womanized* it" (6). However, more than one hundred years before Walker charted Celie's brutalization and her long struggle to free herself, Jacobs womanized the slave narrative when she wrote, "Slavery is terrible for men—but it is far more terrible for women."

2. The nonstandard spelling, punctuation, and grammar of their characters' early letters, which gradually become more standard, are a means by which both Smith and Walker indicate changes from girlhood to womanhood, from ignorance to knowledge. Their characters' displayed mastery of language reflects

self-transformation much as it does in the slave narrative genre. Over the course of time covered by the letters, both Celie and Ivy gain control over "proper" English usage, yet they never abandon their gift for vernacular expression that in a sense frees them from the restrictions that standard language conventions impose. In some ways, like the slave narrators, Celie and Ivy are most themselves when they do not consciously style their words to fit the standards of those who have denied them access to language itself.

3. Adrienne Rich writes of these ceremonies in *Of Woman Born*. Eleusis enshrined the place where "Demeter is supposed to have sat, grieving for the loss of Kôre, and where she returned to establish the ceremonies," which celebrated "reintegration of death and birth, at a time [in history] when patriarchal splitting may have seemed about to sever them entirely" (239).

WORKS CITED

Andrews, William L. *To Tell a Free Story: The First Century of Afro-American Autobiography, 1760–1865.* Urbana: University of Illinois Press, 1986.

Baym, Nina. "Portrayal of Women in American Literature, 1790–1870." In *What Manner of Woman: Essays on English and American Life and Literature,* edited by Marlene Springer, 211–34. New York: New York University Press, 1977.

Belenky, Mary Field, Blythe McVicker Clinchy, Nancy Rule Goldberger, and Jill Mattuck Tarule. *Women's Ways of Knowing: The Development of Self, Voice, and Mind.* New York: Basic Books, 1986.

Bleser, Carol. *The Hammonds of Redcliffe.* New York: Oxford University Press, 1981.

Bush, Trudy Bloser. "Transforming Vision: Alice Walker and Zora Neale Hurston." *Christian Century* (November 16, 1988): 1035–39.

Campbell, Joseph, with Bill Moyers. *The Power of Myth.* New York: Doubleday, 1988.

Carby, Hazel. *Reconstructing Womanhood: The Emergence of the Afro-American Woman Novelist.* New York: Oxford University Press, 1987.

Chesnut, Mary Boykin Miller. *The Private Mary Chesnut: The Unpublished Civil War Diaries.* Edited by C. Vann Woodward and Elisabeth Muhlenfeld. New York: Oxford University Press, 1984.

Christ, Carol P. *Diving Deep and Surfacing: Women Writers on Spiritual Quest,* 2d ed. Boston: Beacon Press, 1986.

Clinton, Catherine. *The Plantation Mistress: Woman's World in the Old South.* New York: Pantheon Books, 1982.

Du Bois, W. E. B. *Darkwater: Voices from Within the Veil.* 1920. Reprint. New York: Schocken Books, 1972.

Dundes, Alan. *Mother Wit from the Laughing Barrel.* Englewood Cliffs, N.J.: Prentice-Hall, 1973.

Faust, Drew Gilpin. *James Henry Hammond and the Old South.* Baton Rouge: Louisiana State University Press, 1982.

Friedman, Jean E. *The Enclosed Garden: Women and Community in the Evangelical South, 1830–1900.* Chapel Hill: University of North Carolina Press, 1985.

Frye, Joanne S. *Living Stories, Telling Lives: Women and the Novel in Contemporary Experience.* Ann Arbor: University of Michigan Press, 1986.

Gilbert, Sandra M., and Susan Gubar. *No Man's Land: The Place of the Woman Writer in the Twentieth Century.* Vol. 1. New Haven: Yale University Press, 1988.

Gilligan, Carol. *In a Different Voice: Psychological Theory and Women's Development.* Cambridge: Harvard University Press, 1982.

Glasgow, Ellen. *Barren Ground.* Garden City, N.Y.: Grosset and Dunlap, 1925.

———. *A Certain Measure: An Interpretation of Prose Fiction.* New York: Harcourt, Brace and Co., 1938.

———. *The Woman Within.* 1954. Reprint. New York: Hill and Wang, 1980.

Gwin, Minrose C. *Black and White Women of the Old South: The Peculiar Sisterhood in American Literature.* Knoxville: University of Tennessee Press, 1985.

Hemenway, Robert. "That Which the Soul Lives By." Introduction to *Mules and Men,* by Zora Neale Hurston, xi–xxviii. Bloomington: Indiana University Press, 1978.

Hernton, Calvin C. *The Sexual Mountain and Black Women Writers: Adventures in Sex, Literature, and Real Life.* New York: Doubleday, 1987.

Holloway, Karla F. C. *The Character of the Word: The Texts of Zora Neale Hurston.* New York: Greenwood Press, 1987.

Hurston, Zora Neale. *Dust Tracks on a Road: An Autobiography.* 1942. 2d ed. Edited with an introduction by Robert E. Hemenway. Urbana: University of Illinois Press, 1984.

———. *Mules and Men.* 1935. Reprint. Bloomington: Indiana University Press, 1978.

———. *Their Eyes Were Watching God.* 1937. Reprint. Urbana: University of Illinois Press, 1978.

Jacobs, Harriet. *Incidents in the Life of a Slave Girl, Written by Herself.* Edited by L. Maria Child. 1861. Reprint. Edited and with an introduction by Jean Fagan Yellin. Cambridge: Harvard University Press, 1987.

Jelinek, Estelle C. "Introduction: Women's Autobiography and the Male Tradition." In *Women's Autobiography: Essays in Criticism,* edited by Estelle C. Jelinek, 1–20. Bloomington: Indiana University Press, 1980.

Jones, Anne Goodwyn. *Tomorrow Is Another Day: The Woman Writer in the South, 1859–1936.* Baton Rouge: Louisiana State University Press, 1981.

Meese, Elizabeth A. *Crossing the Double-Cross: The Practice of Feminist Criticism.* Chapel Hill: University of North Carolina Press, 1986.

Mossberg, Barbara Antonina Clarke. *Emily Dickinson: When a Writer Is a Daughter.* Bloomington: Indiana University Press, 1983.

Olney, James. "'I Was Born': Slave Narratives, Their Status as Autobiography and as Literature." In *The Slave's Narrative,* edited by Charles T. Davis and Henry Louis Gates, Jr., 148–74. New York: Oxford University Press, 1985.

———. "Some Versions of Memory / Some Versions of Bios: The Ontology of Autobiography." In *Autobiography: Essays Theoretical and Critical,* edited by James Olney, 236–67. Princeton: Princeton University Press, 1980.

———. *Metaphors of Self: The Meaning of Autobiography.* Princeton: Princeton University Press, 1972.

Olsen, Tillie. *Silences.* 1965. Reprint. New York: Dell Publishing Co., 1979.

Prenshaw, Peggy Whitman. "The Antiphonies of Eudora Welty's *One Writer's Beginnings* and Elizabeth Bowen's *Pictures and Conversations.*" In *Welty: A Life in Literature,* edited by Albert J. Devlin, 225–37. Jackson: University Press of Mississippi, 1987.

Raper, J. R. *Without Shelter: The Early Career of Ellen Glasgow.* Baton Rouge: Louisiana State University Press, 1971.

Rich, Adrienne. *Of Woman Born: Motherhood as Experience and Institution.* 1976. Reprint with new foreword. New York: Norton, 1986.

———. *Your Native Land, Your Life: Poems.* New York: Norton, 1986.

Rose, Willie Lee. *Slavery and Freedom.* Edited by William W. Freehling. New York: Oxford University Press, 1982.

Scott, Anne Firor. *Southern Lady: From Pedestal to Politics, 1830–1930.* Chicago: University of Chicago Press, 1970.

Sjoo, Monica, and Barbara Mor. *The Great Cosmic Mother: Rediscovering the Religion of the Earth.* San Francisco: Harper and Row, 1987.

Simpson, Lewis P. "The Southern Aesthetic of Memory." *Tulane Studies in English* 23 (1978): 207–27.

Smith, Lee. *Fair and Tender Ladies.* New York: G. P. Putnam's Sons, 1988.

Tiegreen, Helen Hurt. "Mothers, Daughters, and One Writer's Revisions." In *Welty: A Life in Literature,* edited by Albert J. Devlin, 188–211. Jackson: University Press of Mississippi, 1987.

Wagner, Linda W. *Ellen Glasgow: Beyond Convention.* Austin: University of Texas Press, 1982.

Walker, Alice. *The Color Purple.* 1982. Reprint. New York: Washington Square Press, 1983.

———, ed. *I Love Myself When I Am Laughing: A Zora Hurston Reader.* New York: Feminist Press, 1979.

———. *In Search of Our Mothers' Gardens.* New York: Harcourt Brace Jovanovich, 1983.

Welter, Barbara. "The Cult of True Womanhood: 1820–1860." *American Quarterly* 18 (Summer 1966): 151–74.

Welty, Eudora. *One Writer's Beginnings.* Cambridge: Harvard University Press, 1984.

———. *The Optimist's Daughter.* New York: Random House, 1972.

————. *The Ponder Heart.* 1954. Reprint. New York: Harcourt Brace Jovanovich, 1978.

————. "Some Notes on Time in Fiction." In *The Eye of the Story: Selected Essays and Reviews,* 163–73. New York: Random House, 1970.

Westling, Louise. *Sacred Groves and Ravaged Gardens: The Fiction of Eudora Welty, Carson McCullers, and Flannery O'Connor.* Athens: University of Georgia Press, 1985.

White, Deborah Gray. *Ar'n't I a Woman? Female Slaves in the Plantation South.* New York: Norton, 1985.

Willis, Susan. *Specifying: Black Women Writing the American Experience.* Madison: University of Wisconsin Press, 1987.

Wyatt-Brown, Bertram. *Southern Honor: Ethics and Behavior in the Old South.* New York: Oxford University Press, 1982.

Yellin, Jean Fagin. Introduction. In *Incidents in the Life of a Slave Girl, Written by Herself,* by Harriet Jacobs, xiii–xxxiv. Cambridge: Harvard University Press, 1987.

INDEX

Authorship: concepts of Glasgow, Hurston, and Welty, 39–40

Autobiography, 30, 31; of memory, 40–41; chronology in men's vs. women's, 43, 117 (n. 2)

Barnard College, 60

Barren Ground, 7, 12, 67, 68, 69–77, 86–87, 95, 96–97, 100–101, 109, 118 (n. 2), 118–19 (n. 3); natural cycles, 67, 77, 78, 95; romantic love, 70; farming as metaphor, 71; mother's sacrifice, 71–72, 78; Dorinda's masculine clothes, 73, 78, 93; kinship with land, 73–74, 76–77; Demeter legend, 74–75; Jason as death symbol, 75–76; struggle against death, 75–77

Bible, 16, 38, 62; patriarchs in, 15; male heroes in, 39

Billings, John Shaw, 26

Biological determinism: in *Barren Ground* and *Their Eyes Were Watching God*, 77

Boas, Franz, 60–61

Brent, Linda. *See* Jacobs, Harriet

Byer, Kathryn Stripling, 110

Byrd, William, of Westover, 15

Campbell, Joseph, 38, 64, 95

A Certain Measure, 67, 69, 74

Chesnut, Mary B., 15–16

Child, Lydia Maria, 17

Civil War, the, 20–21

The Color Purple, 7, 13, 119 (n. 1); woman's subservient role in, 103–4; letterwriting in, 104–5; Celie's achievement of voice, 105; Celie as matriarch, 108

Cowper, William: "The Task," 34, 116 (n. 9)

Daughter, southern ideal of, 5; 38–39; as writer, 10, 114 (n. 4); Celie and Ivy Rowe as lost daughters, 103; retaining maiden names, 118 (n. 1). *See also* Mother/Daughter bonds

Demeter legend, 65–67, 74–75, 89, 102, 110, 119 (n. 7), 120 (n. 3)

Dreams: Hurston's, in *Dust Tracks*, 56; Dorinda's, in *Barren Ground*, 76; Laurel's, in *The Optimist's Daughter*, 95–96

Du Bois, W. E. B., 21

Dust Tracks on a Dirt Road, 6, 39, 43, 47, 56, 117 (n. 2); early sections of, 43–44; Hurston's organizing visions, 56

Emerson, Ralph Waldo, 4, 5, 13; "Days," 4–5

Evans, Augusta Jane: *St. Elmo*, 3

Fair and Tender Ladies, 7, 13, 110; woman's fate, 105; sisterhood,

Fair and Tender Ladies, (*continued*)
107–8; value of stories, 107–8, 109; letterwriting in, 107–9
Family: southern, 7–8, 10; biblical model, 15–16; demands of, in *Fair and Tender Ladies,* 106–7. *See also* Parental conflict, Patriarchy
Father, the southern, 10; James Henry Hammond as, 22, 24; Samuel Tredwell Sawyer as (in *Incidents in the Life of a Slave Girl*), 35; Glasgow's battle with, 44–46; Hurston's battle of words with, 46–47; influence of Welty's, 47–49, 56–57, 117–18 (n. 5). *See also* Patriarchy

Gardens, 4, 5, 14; mothers', in *The Optimist's Daughter,* 93; Alice Walker's search for, 97
Gender, 7, 8, 9, 11. *See also* Race
Glasgow, Anne Gholson, 45
Glasgow, Ellen, 6, 7, 10, 11, 12, 13, 38, 40–41, 48, 57, 67, 101, 114 (n. 5), 117 (n. 3); sense of vocation, 39, 43–44, 51–53, 55; *Life and Gabriella,* 44; conflicts with father, 44–46, 49–50; mother's influence, 45, 48, 101–2; relations with "Mammy," 52, 100; early novels, 59; return to South as writer, 59–60
Glasgow, Francis, 38, 44–45, 49

Hammond, Catherine Fitzsimons, 6, 7, 13, 16, 17, 18, 36, 37, 64, 66, 99, 116 (nn. 6–7); letters in Bleser collection, 16, 22; life compared to Harriet Jacobs's, 18–22; building

Redcliffe, 20; letters to Marcus Hammond, 22–26; silences, 22, 32; concern for children, 24, 32–33; effect of Civil War on, 24–27; shapes separate identity, 26
Hammond, James Henry, 6, 16, 17, 22–24, 115 (n. 4), 116 (n. 6); death of, 20, 25; patriarchal attitude, 21
Hammond, Julia Bryan, 20
Hammond, Katharine Fitzsimons, 26
Hammond, Marcus, 16, 22–26, 64
Hammond, Spann, 24
Hampton, Wade, 19
Harvard Annex, 20
Heroism: male vs. female versions, 39, 53, 97, 110; women's writing as, 40, 42
Home: South's veneration of, 10; return to, in southern women's novels, 12; Catherine Hammond's, 25–26; woman's place in, 27, 38–39; promise of, in *Incidents in the Life of a Slave Girl,* 27, 31–32, 35–36; Hammond's and Jacobs's leaving and return, 37–38; Ellen Glasgow's in Richmond, 44–45, 59–60; Zora Neale Hurston's in Eatonville, 46, 60–61; Eudora Welty's in Jackson, 47–48, 63; return of Glasgow, Hurston, and Welty to, as writers, 57–63; Celie's in *The Color Purple,* 108; Ivy Rowe's in *Fair and Tender Ladies,* 108–9
Hurston, John, 46–47, 50
Hurston, Lucy, 46–47, 61–62
Hurston, Zora Neale, 6, 7, 11, 12, 13, 38, 40–41, 48, 57, 67, 101, 114 (n. 5), 116 (n. 1), 118 (n. 2); as

storyteller, 41–42, 52–53, 55–56; influence of parents, 46–47, 50; education, 60–61; voice as folklorist, 60–62

Incidents in the Life of a Slave Girl, 19–20, 27–36, 100, 115 (n. 3), 116 (nn. 8–9); character as agent in, 28; title, 28–29; oppositions in, 29–30; selection of incidents, 30–33; use of metaphor, 31, 34, 35, 37–38; double standard in, 32; ending, 35–36
In Search of Our Mothers' Gardens, 97, 103, 110, 115 (n. 6), 116–17 (n. 1)

Jacobs, Harriet, 6, 7, 9, 17–18, 27, 64, 66, 82, 99, 109, 119 (n. 1); achievement of voice, 17, 28, 32; life compared to Catherine F. Hammond's, 18–22; writing autobiography, 19–20; work after Civil War, 20; creates audience, 21; subverting patriarchy, 29, 31–35; explains illegitimate children, 32–33; years of hiding, 33–35; grandmother as matriarch, 35–36; letter to Ednah Dow Cheney, 36, 64–65, 109
Journeys: southern women writers', 6; of Glasgow, Hurston, and Welty, inward, 38, 40, 51–57; connecting inner and outer worlds, 57–63; Welty's definition of, 63; of Dorinda, Janie, and Laurel, 87

Letterwriting, women's, 7; Catherine Hammond's, 6, 22–26; Harriet Jacobs's, 34–35, 36, 64–65, 109; in *The Color Purple,* 104–5; in *Fair and Tender Ladies,* 107, 108, 109; in *The Optimist's Daughter,* 110
Lincoln, Abraham, 20

Matriarchy: southern tradition of, 17–18, 35, 115 (n. 2); Harriet Jacobs's creation of, 31; Dorinda's creation of, in *Barren Ground,* 71, 118–19 (n. 3); Celie's creation of, in *The Color Purple,* 108
Memory, in southern literature, 10, 114 (n. 5); in autobiography, 40–41, 118 (n. 2); in *The Optimist's Daughter,* 68, 95–96; defined by Welty, 96; in *One Writer's Beginnings,* 96–97, 117–18 (n. 5)
Metaphor, 31; in *Incidents in the Life of a Slave Girl,* 31–35; childhood as, 43
Mother/Daughter bonds: in *Incidents in the Life of a Slave Girl,* 35; Glasgow's separation from, 44–45; Hurston's separation from, 46–47; in *Barren Ground,* 71–72; in *The Optimist's Daughter,* 93–94, 110; Alice Walker's search for, 97, 110; Adrienne Rich defines, 98, 100–102, 111; in *Fair and Tender Ladies,* 107–8
Mother Goddess: image of, in Jacobs's and Hammond's writing, 64–66; defined, 65; in southern women's writing, 111. See also Demeter legend
Mothers. See Mother/Daughter bonds
Mother wit, 81, 119 (n. 5)
Mules and Men, 61–62

Naming: Women's, 14, 16, 66, 118
  (n. 1); practices in the South, 15,
  115 (n. 1); Harriet Jacobs's and
  Catherine Hammond's practice of,
  36–38; in *Their Eyes Were
  Watching God,* 81–82; Laurel's, in
  The Optimist's Daughter, 96
National Association of Colored
  Women, 20
Nature: symbolism in southern
  women's novels (Glasgow,
  Hurston, Welty), 67–69; in *Barren
  Ground,* 69–70, 73, 76, 78; in *Their
  Eyes Were Watching God,* 78, 86; in
  The Optimist's Daughter, 93–94, 95
Norcom, James, 6, 17, 18, 27–28,
  115–16 (n. 5)
Novel: as feminist form, 12; character
  as agent in, 12–13; plot selection
  in, 30; southern women's, 67

Of Women Born, 98, 100
Olney, James, 31, 40, 116 (n. 8)
Olsen, Tillie: *Silences,* 21–22
One Writer's Beginnings, 3, 4, 6, 39,
  49; as autobiography of memory,
  40–41, 63; ordering of, 42–44, 62,
  117 (n. 2); movement from silence
  to connected knowing, 62–63
The Optimist's Daughter, 7, 12, 86–97,
  100–101, 110, 118 (n. 2); cycles in,
  67–68; Laurel as artist, 86–88;
  return home, 88, 90–91; Demeter
  legend, 88–89, 93; time in, 88–90;
  Fay's role, 91–93; mother's gifts,
  93–94; natural processes in, 94;
  power of memory, 94–96

Parental conflict: in Glasgow's life,
  44–46, 49–50; in Hurston's life,
  46–47, 50; in Welty's life, 47–49,
  50, 51, 54–55
Patriarchy: southern, 5, 6, 11–12, 15–
  16, 26–27; power to limit women's
  identity, 7–8; effect on women's
  interracial communities, 8–10; in
  Jacobs's and Hammond's worlds,
  16–18, 36; in *Incidents in the Life of
  a Slave Girl,* 28, 29, 31–35, 114
  (n. 4), 115 (n. 2); Ellen Glasgow's
  idea of, 38–39, 59
The Ponder Heart, 2–5; Edna Earle as
  southern daughter, 2; subversive
  voice in, 2–3

Race: relation to women's sense of
  community in the South, 8, 9–10;
  separates and links experience of
  Hammond and Jacobs, 18–21, 99;
  Adrienne Rich's analysis of, 98–99;
  in novels of Glasgow, Hurston, and
  Welty, 99–100. *See also* Patriarchy,
  Slavery
Rich, Adrienne, 98–102, 110–11, 120
  (n. 3); "Education of a Novelist,"
  99–100

Sawyer, Samuel Tredwell, 18, 32
Self-definition: in southern women's
  writing, 6–7, 58; autobiographies
  of Glasgow, Hurston, and Welty,
  41–44; Dorinda's (*Barren Ground*)
  achievement of, 76–77; Janie's
  (*Their Eyes Were Watching God*)
  achievement of, 85–86; Laurel's
  (*The Optimist's Daughter*)
  achievement of, 94–97
Silence: southern women's, 4; and

secrecy, for Jacobs and Hammond, 16–17; Catherine Hammond's sentence to, 22, 24–25, 32; Glasgow associates deafness with, 59; Hurston's fear of, 60; Janie's retreat into, in *Their Eyes Were Watching God*, 82, 83; Celie's, in *The Color Purple*, 104–5

Simpson, Lewis: "The Southern Aesthetic of Memory," 10, 114–15 (n. 5)

Sisterhood: defining connection for modern southern women writers, 4, 99; in *The Color Purple* and *Fair and Tender Ladies*, 102–9

Slave narratives, 28–30, 35, 82, 116 (n. 8), 119–20 (nn. 1–2)

Slavery: in the South, 6, 25, 30; black women's experience of, 19, 21, 29, 32, 82, 99

Smith, Lee, 13, 102, 110, 119–20 (n. 2)

"Some Notes on Time in Fiction," 88, 114 (n. 5), 117–18 (n. 5)

South: as patriarchal culture, 5–6, 7–10, 57–58; characteristics of, 10, 114 (n. 3); Glasgow's analysis of, 60

Storytelling: southern women's, 5–6, 7, 55; agency for self-definition, 13–14; men's domination of, in *Dust Tracks*, 41–42; Glasgow begins, 52; Hurston begins, 53–54, 56; as form of leaving home, 55–57; relation to voice in *One Writer's Beginnings*, 56–57; in *Mules and Men*, 61–62; in *Their Eyes Were Watching God*, 68, 84–86, 110; in *The Optimist's Daughter*, 93;

importance for Ivy in *Fair and Tender Ladies*, 107–8, 109

Their Eyes Were Watching God, 7, 12, 67, 77–86, 87, 95, 96–97, 100–101, 109–10, 118 (nn. 1–2), 119 (nn. 4–6); seasonal cycles in, 67–68, 78; Janie's masculine clothes, 78–79, 93; frame narrator's voice, 78–80, 86; Demeter legend in, 79; title, 80–81; language of, 81–83; Nanny (grandmother) as slave narrator, 82–83; Janie's loss of voice in marriage, 83–84; Janie as storyteller, 84–86; creating community of women, 85; natural change, 86

Time: manipulated by southern women autobiographers (Glasgow, Hurston, Welty), 42–43, 68; in *One Writer's Beginnings*, 50, 54, 117 (n. 5); Glasgow's sense of in *Barren Ground*, 67–68; in *The Optimist's Daughter*, 68–69, 88–92

True Womanhood, 9, 27, 29, 113 (n. 2)

Turner, Nat: rebellion, 30

Voice: southern woman's, 1, 6, 13–14, 51, 53, 58, 67, 97, 111; in *The Ponder Heart*, 2; defined, 4, 113 (n. 1); counteracting silence, 10–11, 57–58; Catherine Hammond's 16; Jacobs and Hammond define tradition of, 36; Glasgow's, Hurston's, and Welty's childhood creation of, 51–57; as connecting strategy for Glasgow, Hurston, and Welty, 57–59, 62, 63; Hurston's, in

Voice: southern woman's, (*continued*)
   Mules and Men, 61; Janie's, in *Their
   Eyes Were Watching God,* 78–79;
   mythic dimensions of, 96–97;
   Celie's acts of, in *The Color Purple,*
   104–5

Walker, Alice, 13, 97, 102–3, 107, 118
   (n. 2), 119–20 (n. 2)
Welty, Christian, 47–49, 54
Welty, Eudora, 6, 7, 10, 11, 12, 13,
   38, 40–41, 67, 101, 114 (n. 5);
   writer's vocation, 42, 53–57;
   parents' influence, 47–49, 50–51;
   ambivalence about family, 50–51;

journeys, inward vs. outward, 56–
   57; as "constructive" knower,
   62–63
Willis, Nathaniel P., 19
Woman: Emerson's ideal, 4–5
The Woman Within, 6, 38–39, 41, 43,
   44, 58–60; "prodigal daughter" in,
   38–39; Glasgow's purposes for, 41,
   58; early sections of, 43–44
Women's literature: of the 1850s, 32
Women's Ways of Knowing, 10, 57–58,
   113 (n. 1)
Writing. *See* Storytelling, Voice

Your Native Land, Your Life, 99